How to Succeed as a Freelance Translator

Second Edition

Corinne McKay

How to Succeed as a Freelance Translator, Second Edition
by Corinne McKay

ISBN 978-0-578-07756-7

Disclaimer: This book is published by Two Rat Press and TranslateWrite, Inc., who acknowledge all trademarks. All information contained in this book is believed to be correct at the time of printing. However, readers are advised to seek professional advice where necessary, as the information in this book is based on the author's experiences. The author of this book is not professionally engaged in providing legal, financial or career planning advice. Please send comments or corrections to corinne@translatewrite.com.

Author photograph: Cameron Weise/Colorado Photo
Cover design: Brandon Kellogg/Superfluent Design
Layout and copyediting: Daniel J. Urist

Contents

Introduction to the second edition

Since the first edition of *How to Succeed as a Freelance Translator* was published in 2006, the world economy has undergone some major upheavals, but the translation industry is still a great place to be. The United States Bureau of Labor Statistics predicts that for the 2008-2018 decade, "employment of interpreters and translators is projected to increase 22 percent, much faster than the average for all occupations." `http://www.bls.gov/oco/ocos175.htm#outlook` The United States government's lack of foreign language speakers has been cited as an issue needing immediate action, and President Obama has gone on the record saying, "We should have every child speaking more than one language." Thanks to the ever-increasing volume of global business documentation and communications, translators with excellent language and business skills are still in high demand; despite the global economic downturn, various surveys show that fully three quarters of freelance translators still feel that their business volume is satisfactory or better.

Not surprisingly, the translation industry itself has undergone some major changes in recent years. The translation environment tool (TenT)/computer-assisted translation (CAT) industry has seen the emergence of some new software applications and radical redesigns of other applications, more translators have started incorporating machine translation (MT) into their work, and more corporations have looked to crowdsourcing as an alternative to paying individual translators or translation companies. Small translation companies have been bought by larger ones, and in general it seems that more translators are interested in improving their business skills and working for direct clients. Web 2.0 tools

9

such as blogs, podcasts and online networking have become an indispensable part of the translator's tool kit. In a profession that dates back to antiquity, things are still changing, and changing fast.

The good news about virtual work

In publicizing their work-from-home newsletter *The Rat Race Rebellion*, the e-entrepreneurship specialists Staffcentrix `http://staffcentrix.com` estimate that "There is a 30 to 1 scam ratio among home-based work 'opportunities.' " Although there are definitely some unscrupulous translation clients out there, translation itself is a great example of a legitimate work-from-home opportunity. The vast majority of translators in the U.S. work from home, so translation agencies are used to this business model and don't think it's odd to employ translators who work from home. Home-based work has many advantages for you as the worker, and for your community as a whole. By working from home, you'll probably experience greater job satisfaction and less stress, since a relatively minor disruption like a dentist appointment or furnace repair won't derail your entire work day. Most of the time, you'll be able to structure your work day around your peak energy times and your family's needs, rather than your employer's policies. Your commute will be as long as it takes you to walk from your bedroom to your office and fire up the computer while still in your pajamas. Not surprisingly, most home workers experience a greatly improved quality of life.

Likewise, working from home has a very positive effect on your community and the world as a whole. Less commuting means less traffic congestion, less fuel usage and less need for parking areas. Home-based workers are around during the day, allowing them to volunteer for school and community activities and to be available for their families. A study by the International Telework Association and Council (ITAC) found that home-based workers are absent from work less than half as often as office-based workers, leading to greater work productivity in general.

Is freelance translation for you?

Despite all of these positive aspects, it's very important to do some realistic self-assessment to determine if a career as a freelance translator is right for you. Being bilingual is certainly a translator's key skill, but it isn't enough. Translators also need to know the terminology of their fields of specialization, they need to be proficient in the technology that the industry uses and they need to be excellent writers in their target language.

Equally important, and the subject that we'll focus on in this book, is a translator's ability to run a business. When you work full time for an employer, you have one job title. When you work for yourself, you're not only the translator, but also the department head for sales and marketing, technical support, customer relations, accounting and facilities maintenance. Unless you're willing and able to pay someone to do these tasks for you, you'll be doing them yourself, in addition to your regular job.

Before you launch yourself into a translation career, it's important to ask yourself a few questions. Are you the type of person who is often described as highly motivated, driven, a go-getter; or do you have trouble following through on a plan once the exciting idea stage is over? Are you consistently able to meet deadlines with almost no supervision or direction, or do you head off to shopping websites as soon as the boss disappears? Do you have the multi-tasking skills necessary to manage multiple clients and deadlines at once, or does this type of work leave you feeling overwhelmed and wondering where to start?

It's important to factor in a start-up period of at least six months to a year when launching your freelance business. Of course this is just an estimate, and the length of everyone's start-up period will vary, but for translators who work in a relatively common language pair (for example French, Italian, German, Spanish or Portuguese paired with English), it's best to budget on at least six months of doing a lot of marketing and translating less than full-time. For some people, such as parents of small children or full-time students who are looking for some supplemental income, the spotty cash flow of a start-up period may not be a huge concern.

If you're planning on translation as your full-time income, you'll need to either continue your current employment while your translation business gets up to speed, or plan on living off your savings or a loan during this time. It can help to focus on the fact that with a consistent and reasonably aggressive marketing effort, you'll have years to enjoy your freelance lifestyle and income after your start-up phase ends.

In the 21st century, translators and computers are an inseparable pair, if not always a harmonious one. Anyone with excellent technical skills has a leg up on the average beginning freelance translator, and if you're a dyed-in-the-wool technophobe, it's time to brush up. Technology is probably one of the most overlooked aspects of working as a translator, and one that can be a big factor in a client's willingness to work with you on a regular basis.

The first edition of *How to Succeed as a Freelance Translator* sold over 4,000 copies in its four year print run. I'm excited about releasing this fully updated second edition and hope that it will prove equally helpful to translators around the world!

Acknowledgments and thanks

One of the best parts of being a translator is that translators and writers are such interesting people to know and work with. Many thanks to all of my friends and colleagues who helped this book grow from an idea to a first edition to a second edition: Eve Lindemuth Bodeux has been my translation and brainstorming partner and close friend for the better part of a decade and believed in this book when it was just a back-burner idea; Beth Hayden dragged me into the world of blogging and knew that I would love it; Lillian Clementi, Chris Durban, Judy Jenner, Dierk Seeburg, Melanie Shepherd, Jill Sommer and Jane Wolfrum are some of my most trusted and inspiring colleagues and Karen Mitchell is my writing idol. Thanks also to Eve Lindemuth Bodeux, Mary David of the American Translators Association, S. Patrick Eaton, George Fletcher, Michael Haaren of the Rat Race Rebellion, Grant Hamilton, Jonathan Hine, Judy and Dagmar Jenner, Michelle Vranizan Rafter, Fabio Said, Riccardo Schiaffino, Jill Sommer, Karen Tkaczyk and Jost Zetzsche for their reviews, articles and promotion of the first edition of this book, and to Terena Bell, Marian Greenfield, Tom Hedden and Freek Lankhof for their suggestions for the second edition. And the sometimes isolating world of the home office would be much less appealing without our vibrant local group, the Colorado Translators Association; I feel fortunate to have this network of colleagues right outside my door.

My parents taught me to love books and seeing the world. My daughter's enthusiasm for life inspires me to keep on learning and creating, and my husband has a way of fixing almost everything. To paraphrase P.G. Wodehouse, without them this book would have been finished in half the time, but I love them all the more for it.

13

1 An overview of the translation business

1.1 What is a translator?

In a nutshell, a translator is a human being who changes written words from one language to another. If this sounds obvious, take another look! First, it's important to note that although computers play an important role in translation, professional translators are humans, not computers. Second, a translator works with written words, unlike an interpreter, who works with spoken words. If you're new to the industry, you've learned something important right here; that the phrase "speaking through a translator," contradicts itself, since translators work in writing. While some people work as both translators and interpreters, most concentrate on one or the other.

Translators are also, by definition, fluent in more than one language. In the industry, these are referred to as the *source*, or "from" language(s), and the *target*, or "into" language, which is almost always the translator's native language. So for example, a translator who is a native English speaker and learned Portuguese and Spanish might translate from Spanish and Portuguese into English. In the United States, the translation market is heavily geared toward translators who work into their native language.

If you work in a less common language pair, you might find yourself as the exception to this rule. A client might need a document translated from Thai into English, a job that would usually be handled by a native English speaker who has Thai as a second or third language. However in practice, it's often easier to find a native Thai speaker who has English as a second language since there are many more native Thai speakers who also speak

English than the other way around. In this case, the job might be handled by a native Thai speaker, and then proofread by a native English speaker.

In the United States, most translators work in a small number of languages. Most have only one primary language pair. This is the norm in the U.S. but can be a handicap for translators who want to work or go to graduate school in Europe, where it is much more common for translators to work from at least two languages.

1.2 What does it take to become a translator?

Being multilingual isn't the only skill a translator needs, but it's certainly the most important. Translators learn their languages in many different ways; many grew up in bilingual households or countries, some learned their second or third language in school and then pursued experience abroad, some took intensive language courses or worked in a foreign country for several years, and many translators have become freelancers after working as military or government linguists.

Almost all translators working in the U.S. have at least a Bachelor's Degree, although not necessarily in translation. As a rule, most professional translators have at least some experience working and/or living in a country where their source language(s) are spoken; many translators lived and worked in their source language country for many years, or pursued higher education in their source language(s). In-country experience is a big asset for a translator, since translation work involves knowing not just the structure of the language to be translated, but the cultural framework that surrounds it. Classroom study can make you very proficient in a language but in order to translate successfully, you need *near-native* proficiency in your source language(s). If you're starting from scratch, a few semesters of part-time language class won't be enough. As a point of reference, the U.S. Government's Defense Language Institute Foreign Language Center offers a program to teach Middle Eastern languages to government employees, and the *basic* program involves 63 weeks of full time study.

Many people wonder how to tell if their language skills are good enough to work as a translator. While there are various language testing services that can tell you where you stand, probably the easiest way to get a feel for your translation readiness is to translate something. Go on the web and find a legal document, newspaper article or press release in your source language, then translate it and ask a professional translator to review your work. The key points are: can you understand this document on both a word-for-word and a conceptual level, and can you convey its meaning in your target language? Members of the American Translators Association can also take the practice test for the ATA certification exam if it is offered in their language pair.

Translators today work in almost every conceivable language pair; while the market in the United States has historically been very strong in high-volume languages such as French, German, Italian, Portuguese and Spanish, there is a large (and increasingly lucrative) market for translation in Chinese, Japanese, Arabic, Russian the Nordic languages and the "languages of smaller diffusion" like Nepali, Hebrew and Somali. In most language pairs, the amount of work available is proportionate to the number of translators in the language. There is a lot of English to Spanish translation work available in the U.S., but the quantity of available English to Spanish translators causes increased competition and possibly lower rates. The reverse is true of smaller-diffusion languages.

In addition to near-native knowledge of their source language(s), translators need other skills too; probably the most important are excellent writing skills in their target language, in-depth knowledge in one or more areas of specialization, and business management skills. Some would-be translators struggle because they are not good writers in their native language. Highly specialized translators are among the highest-earning members of the profession; for example a bilingual intellectual property attorney, stock broker or biomedical engineer may earn many times the per-word rate of a "jack of all trades" translator with a B.A. in

German. Some translators turn a previous career into an area of specialization, while others take additional courses in areas of specialization or learn specialized terminology from more experienced translators. Paradoxically, specializing can lead to more work, not less, as the specialized translator becomes known as the go-to person in his or her area of expertise, whether it's environmental engineering, textile manufacturing or stage sets.

The translation industry in the U.S. is firmly based on the independent contractor model. There are some in-house translation jobs, for example in English to Spanish translation or for U.S. government agencies such as the FBI and CIA. Since most translators are self-employed freelancers, business skills are critical to your survival in the industry. You might be an outstanding translator, but if you can't market yourself, meet deadlines, keep track of your billings and keep your technology setup up to date, you will find yourself struggling to make a healthy income.

1.3 Improving your language skills

If you'd like to work as a translator but your language skills are not yet up to par, you have a few options. The best is immersion: living and working or going to school in a country where your source language is spoken. If you are not in a position to work or study overseas, most colleges and universities in the U.S. have foreign language classes and some (although far fewer than in most other countries) have translation and interpreting classes.

If you're trying to improve your language skills, be realistic; although it's certainly not impossible to learn a new language as an adult, it's also not going to happen with a few semesters of night classes. If you're starting from a beginner level or close to it, two to three years of intensive language study in a college-level program is probably a bare minimum.

1.4 A translator's working environment

The translation industry in the United States is heavily geared toward self-employed independent contractors (freelance translators). In the past, many large companies and even many translation agencies had staffs of in-house translators, but these jobs are now rare, and when they do exist would rarely be given to a beginner. In contrast to other professions where newcomers are expected to pay their dues as in-house employees and then enjoy the "reward" of freelancing, the translation industry usually works in the opposite way. Most translators start out as freelancers and may remain self-employed for their whole careers, while most well-paid in-house translators are hired with years or even decades of experience. It's important to be realistic about whether the life of a freelancer is for you. While you'll have a great degree of control over where, when and how much you work, you'll also give up the security of a steady paycheck, benefits, paid time off, and a pension or employer-sponsored 401K.

Most freelance translators in the U.S. work from a home office, and there is no stigma attached to working from home; translators who rent office space outside the home are definitely the exception rather than the rule. The vast majority of a translator's work is done on the computer, using either a word processing program or text editor, and possibly a computer-assisted translation program. Translators make extensive use of reference materials such as print and online dictionaries, terminology databases, and discussion with other translators. The almost constant use of a computer makes repetitive strain injury one of the few work-related injuries that translators are at risk for.

There are many positive sides to a translator's work environment. Compared to other work-from-home jobs, translation can be very interesting and well-paying. Translation industry compensation surveys report that the average self-employed freelance translator earns over $60,000 per year, and income of over $100,000 seems to be the new normal for translators who work primarily with direct clients or who work in high-demand language pairs or specializations.

As you would expect, it takes a lot of time, effort and some luck to reach that level of income. Before starting your freelance translation business, you'll need to determine if you have the financial resources, time and energy to get through the startup period to the point where you are earning a reasonable and steady income. Everyone's start-up phase is different, but most freelancers take between six and eighteen months to build up a base of regular clients.

Starting a translation business is a fairly inexpensive proposition in terms of capital (not in terms of time!). If you already have a home computer and high speed Internet access, you might make do with business cards, membership in your local translators association and a modest reference library, for a startup cost of only a few hundred dollars.

Freelance translation is relatively location-independent, meaning that you can work from almost anywhere that you can get a high-speed Internet connection. In addition, most translators can work on fairly flexible schedule; it's nice to be able to work at the times of day when you are the most productive. Freelance translation is a great job for people who want to devote time to their families or other non-work interests since translators can work whenever they want as long as they meet their deadlines.

On the downside (and of course there are some downsides to all of this!), as with other consulting or freelance work, some aspects of translation can be stressful and difficult to manage. Many translators describe their work as feast or famine, with months of little to no work and months of too much work. Worldwide business acceleration has affected translation turnaround times and clients often want projects turned around as fast as possible. Clients who pay late or don't pay at all can cause major financial problems, especially for translators who live paycheck to paycheck. Translators who work in common language combinations like Spanish↔English may face pressure to lower their rates in order to remain competitive, especially if the client can find qualified translators in countries where pay rates are much lower. In addition, working from home has its ups and downs; even for an introvert, the life of the home office can be lonely, and time spent on (unpaid) non-translation work like accounting, marketing and maintaining computer systems can become frustrating when you'd much rather be translating! Succeeding as a translator demands a high degree of self-discipline in order to force yourself to meet your deadlines with no boss in the next cubicle.

However, once you have a base of regular clients and find the types of translation work that you enjoy doing, you can really reap the rewards of all that marketing and research. The translation industry is growing much faster than the pool of qualified translators, so it's an excellent industry to break into.

1.5 What kinds of work do translators do?

As cross-cultural and multilingual communication become more important to the worldwide flow of business, translators and interpreters are employed in almost every conceivable business and government sector. From law to health care to finance, entertainment, information technology and advertising, translators and interpreters enable global communication. Some translators, especially those with specialized professional or technical training, might concentrate on only one subject area, such as pharmaceuticals, corporate finance, computer software or legal contracts. There are even translators who specialize in seemingly obscure areas like fisheries management, shopping mall construction, stamps, or groundwater hydrology. Still others position themselves as general translators with concentrations in certain areas. The more common your language pair, the more important it is to specialize in order to find your niche in the market.

Translators sometimes work with a partner or in groups, particularly on large projects that need to be turned around quickly. Today, translation teams almost always work together over the Internet, rather than in person. The size of translation projects can vary widely, from a single line of text such as a company slogan, to an entire book or website. Most translators who are self-employed work from project to project, with the average project taking anywhere from an hour to several days, and some longer projects mixed in as well.

Although most translators in the U.S. are independent contractors, full time jobs for translators and interpreters do exist, particularly in areas such as court and health care interpreting, web content translation, software localization, and translating and interpreting for the United States Government's various agencies including the Federal Bureau of Investigation, Central Intelligence Agency and National Security Agency. Translators who are experienced and/or qualified to work in more than one language pair may have a greater chance of being offered an in-house position.

Literary translators (translators who work on books, poetry or short stories) make up a relatively small segment of translators in the United States. This is because literary translation is typically not very well paid, and because Americans don't tend to read literature in translation, so there is a small market for the work of literary translators; approximately 3% of books published in the United States are translations. If you translate into a language other than English, there may be a larger market for literary translation services, especially if you are qualified to work on textbooks, technical manuals, and other "non-literary" book projects.

Localization translators are a rapidly growing group in the industry. Localization, or the complete adaptation of a product such as a web site, product marketing kit, software program or advertising campaign into another language, used to be confined mostly to computer software. Now, software localization is probably the largest segment of the localization market, but it's certainly not the only segment. Businesses may hire localization agencies when they want to take a new product global and need culturally-targeted marketing advice in addition to translation services.

1.5.1 Translation

By definition, translation, the process of changing written material from one language to another, is a translator's core business activity. A few pointers here: unless you truly consider yourself

to be a native speaker of two languages, you should be translating into your native language only, not into your second or
third language. There are certainly exceptions to this, for example in small-diffusion languages where translators are hard to
find. However if you work in English paired with a commonly
translated language such as French, Italian, German, Spanish or
Portuguese, stick to translating into your native language only.
Translation is most often paid by the word, in some countries
(specifically Germany) by the line, and less often by the hour.
Some tasks within the industry, such as editing and proofreading,
are more frequently paid by the hour. Make sure to clarify ahead
of time whether your client will be paying you by the source or
target word count, since these can differ by as much as 30%.

1.5.2 Editing

Translation-specific editing is a skill in its own right, which requires not just knowledge of the source and target language of
the document to be edited, but also of the spelling, grammar and
usage conventions of the target language. Editing (also sometimes
called revising) is sometimes reserved for experienced translators,
but if you enjoy editing it's worth offering it as an additional
service. If you would like to offer editing services, consider taking
some courses in editing that are specific to your target language.
Editing is paid either by the word or by the hour, which has its
pluses and minuses. If you charge by the hour, you know that you
will be paid for all the time you put in on the project. Charging
by the word will make your client happy because they will get
a fixed quote before you begin the project; the only danger of
charging by the word is that you can end up with a poor hourly
rate if the translation requires extensive revision.

1.5.3 Proofreading

Proofreading can mean two different things: editing a bilingual
document (see above) or proofreading the target document without looking at the source document. Make sure that you clarify

what your client is expecting when you accept a proofreading job.

1.5.4 Voiceover

Voiceover work is an additional service you may want to offer, especially if you live in your source language country and therefore have less competition. Voiceover work can take various forms. Your voice might be used to dub the voice of another person (for example in a television news broadcast) or on its own (for example as the voice track of an advertisement, or as the voice prompts for a phone system). Some voiceover work may even require people who speak with a specific accent. While voiceover work has traditionally been done in recording studios, this is changing as digital technology becomes cheaper and more widely available. It may be possible to record voiceovers from home, especially if you have the funds to set up a small studio. Voiceover work is normally paid by the hour and is handled both by translation agencies and by dedicated voiceover companies.

1.5.5 Transcription

Transcription, which involves making a written transcript of an audio or video recording, is another service that can be done from a home office. Although transcription work may not pay as much as translation, there is a strong market for transcription in English and in other languages. Some translators also offer "on the fly" transcription/translation, where the translator listens to an audio recording and instead of making a transcript in the source language, translates while listening to the audio and produces a written document in the target language. If you would like to offer transcription services and you will be working from an electronic file (as opposed to a CD or tape), it is helpful to have specialized playback software that allows you to control the audio file from your keyboard.

1.5.6 On-site document review

Some translation clients, such as law firms or financial services companies, may have cases or business dealings that require them to review large volumes of foreign language documents in a short period of time. On-site document review, where the translator goes to the client's office to summarize the content of those documents either verbally or in writing, can result in dramatic time and cost savings for these clients. After you have identified the general subject matter or content of the documents, the client can then decide which documents, if any, need to be translated. On-site document review is usually billed by the hour; large corporations in major cities are the best prospects for this type of work.

1.5.7 Machine translation post-editing

Machine translation, translation that is done entirely by a computer, is becoming an increasingly important factor in the translation industry. Most machine translation requires post-editing by a human before it can be published or distributed. Some translators really enjoy this type of work and others despise it, but many companies feel that experienced translators make the best post-editors. Post-editing can be paid by the word or by the hour.

1.5.8 Software localization

An additional sub-specialty within the translation and localization industry is software localization, the process of translating software code and user interfaces from one language to another. For example, when a large software company produces multilingual versions of its applications, every piece of text displayed by the software must be translated into the target language, and in many cases the graphics must be altered as well. Software localization involves both bilingual software developers and document translators specialized in information technology, since the software's user interface, help files, readme files, screen shots and incidental files (such as warranty information and packaging) must all be translated.

Software localization is an enormous industry in its own right, largely because computer users throughout the world now expect their software to be in their own language, and will naturally be more interested in purchasing software or visiting websites that they can access in their own language. Localization breeds localization; a localized web browser automatically creates a need for localized websites; a localized piece of software demands a localized manual to go with it.

1.6 Who do translators work for?

1.6.1 Working for translation agencies

For a freelance translator, there are typically two types of clients: *translation agencies* and *direct clients*. First, let's look at how translators work through agencies. A translation agency, which may also refer to itself as a *language services provider*, *translation company*, or *translation bureau*, has its own roster of clients and sub-contracts their translation work to individual freelance translators. The agency handles the project management end of things, interacts directly with the translation client and (hopefully) pays the translator and deals with any collections issues. Ideally, the translation agency should pay its freelance translators when their invoices come due (normally 30 days after the agency accepts the translation) whether the agency itself has been paid by the end client or not.

In the uncertain world of freelancing, translation agencies provide some measure of job security. Your regular agency clients may keep you very busy, and allow you to focus on translating rather than on answering the end client's questions or dealing with billing and collections. Reputable agencies should pay you regardless of whether the end client pays them. In addition, marketing to agencies is relatively easy and is much less time-consuming than marketing to direct clients. Translators who work for agencies are also relatively free to pick and choose their assignments. You don't want to turn down too much work from an agency client, but it's also unlikely that they will refuse to work with you if you decline their projects once in a while. Agencies also generally have more than one translator per language pair or specialization, so they may be able to find a backup translator if you get sick or have a family emergency. Many of these safety net components are up to you to figure out when you work with direct clients!

In exchange for this level of stability, the agency will pay you as little as half of what the end client pays them. They may also decline to let you communicate directly with the end client if you have questions about the translation, and they may require you to sign a non-disclosure or non-competition agreement in which you agree not to accept or solicit work directly from the end client. Some agencies, especially large ones, may pressure their translators to lower their rates in order to win large volumes of work.

Before you apply to agencies, decide what tradeoffs you are willing to make in order to work with them. If you just want to translate and you're not interested in marketing, collecting or building the relationships that lead to direct client work, agencies can be a good option. If you will be driven crazy by the fact that the agency is earning a good deal of profit on your translation, simply find another business model.

1.6.2 Working for direct clients

Many freelance translators also work for direct clients, meaning that the business relationship is between the freelancer and the client with no intermediary involved. There are direct clients in nearly any business sector you can imagine: finance, law, IT, patents, education, travel and tourism and an endless list of others. The income potential of working for direct clients is attractive; in many cases double the income of working for an agency. Direct clients may also be able to provide large volumes of work if their turnaround time allows for it. Whereas a translation agency will often split a large project between several translators to get it done faster, a direct client might be more interested in consistency than in turnaround time. A direct client might also be willing to let you act as a "mini-agency," subcontracting work to other translators you know and keeping a percentage for yourself. With a direct client the translator is often more in control of the payment terms involved; for example, the translator might be able to request payment in advance for certain services, an option that almost never exists when working through a translation agency.

There are some disadvantages in working for direct clients as well. When you work through an agency, it's the project manager's job to explain the ins and outs of the translation process to the client. If the client doesn't know what source and target language mean, or the difference between traditional and simplified Chinese, or whether they want the company's name in all capital letters throughout the document, it's the agency's responsibility to deal with this, not yours. When you work for a direct client, for better or worse there's no one between you and the client. If the client has an unrealistic deadline, keeps changing his/her mind about the project specifications, or wants additional services such as desktop publishing, it's up to you as the translator to deal with it. If the direct client doesn't pay, there's no one else to lean on for the money— you simply have to handle it yourself, or hire a collection agency if things turn really sour. All of these aspects are worth considering before you decide whether to work through agencies or for direct clients.

1.7 A bit about interpreting

As you explore a career in translation (written language work), consider whether you would like to focus your business exclusively on translation, or include interpreting (spoken language work) in your range of services. Like translation, the market for interpreting depends largely on your language pair(s). Interpreting can be more location-dependent than translation; unless you do over-the-phone interpreting, you need to either find clients in your location or go to where your clients are.

Interpreting has several "modes," the primary ones being *simultaneous*, where the interpreter talks at the same time as the speaker; *consecutive*, where the interpreter listens to the speaker and takes notes, then interprets what the speaker said; and *sight translation*, where the interpreter reads a written document in another language, for example taking a court document in English and reading it to a defendant in Spanish. Simultaneous interpreting is probably the most common mode, since it is used in diplomatic settings, in court and in various conference settings.

Interpreting demands very different skills than translation. While translators are stereotypically detail-oriented introverts who don't mind spending an hour finding the perfect translation for a word, interpreters must be able to think on their feet and work with little or no advance preparation. Translators most often work alone at home, while interpreters are literally in the spotlight, standing next to a court witness, hospital patient or head of state and communicating for him or her.

Until the advent of conference calling, interpreters had to be in the same place as their clients, and court and conference interpreting is still heavily dependent on on-site interpreters. However, over-the-phone interpreting is becoming more popular, especially in areas where it's hard to find on-site interpreters. Many translation agencies also handle interpreting clients; and courts, hospitals and schools may employ in-house interpreters.

One major difference between interpreting and translation is that interpreters often work in both "directions" of their language pair, so must be highly proficient in speaking their non-native language; many high-level conference interpreters consider themselves to have two native languages, rather than one native language and one or more second languages. Interpreters are paid by the hour or by the day, and pay varies widely. In some areas of the U.S., English↔Spanish court interpreters might make less than $15 an hour, while experienced conference interpreters might make $700 a day or more.

If you are interested in interpreting, one excellent way to assess your skills is to go spend a day as an observer in court. Most courts in the U.S. are open to the public, and you can sit in the viewing area and try to interpret as the proceedings go along; better yet take a notebook and make a list of words and expressions that you need to research. The major employers of full-time interpreters in the U.S. are courts, the health care industry and schools, so these are all good places to focus on if you would like to explore interpreting work. You might also consider "shadowing" an interpreter who works in your language pair; just make sure to be unobtrusive and thank the interpreter for her/his time and expertise.

1.8 How do translators set their rates?

Translators are most commonly paid by the word, with some variation in whether the word count is based on the source or target language, though the convention varies by country. In the U.S., translators are usually paid per single word, but in the U.K. payment is usually per thousand words. In Germany, payment is commonly made by the 55-character line.

Translators may charge by the hour for projects where a per-word rate does not reflect the amount of work that the project requires, for example translating advertising slogans and marketing materials. Translations of official documents such as birth certificates may be billed by the page. Many translators have a minimum charge for small projects, for example a flat fee for projects up to 250 words. It's also common for translators to add a premium for a rush project, or to offer a discount for a large project or ongoing work.

The actual per-word rate depends on your language combination(s) and specialization(s), and also on what your clients are willing to pay. Asking "How much do translators charge?" is like asking, "How big is a ball of yarn?" The variation in translation rates is enormous; the low end of the market is translators who work for free or for just a few cents a word, and the very high end is in the range of 40-50 cents a word.

1.8.1 Charging by the word versus charging by the hour

Translators have traditionally charged by the word, with editors charging either by the word or by the hour. This way of billing has various advantages and disadvantages for both translators/editors and their clients.

On the pro side, charging by the word, especially by the source word, means that everyone knows in advance how much the translation will cost. A 10,000 word translation at 20 cents per word will cost exactly $2,000, no matter how long it takes the translator to complete it. Charging by the word is also an advantage for experienced translators and those who keep up with advances in translation productivity software, since translators who work faster make more money. Finally, charging by the word leaves very little room for debate or interpretation about what work is billable and what work is not; the translator simply issues an invoice for the number of words translated (just make sure to always agree in advance on whether you will bill for the source or target word count).

On the con side, charging by the word commits the translator to a flat rate for the project no matter how long it takes. In the example above, whether it takes you 20 hours to translate 10,000 words of straightforward text with very little to look up and no complex formatting, or 40 hours to translate complex tables and barely legible handwritten text, you still earn the same $2,000. As discussed above, charging by the hour also leads to room for debate over what is billable and what is not. For example, should the translator bill for reading and responding to the client's e-mails? Talking to the project manager on the phone? Proofreading the document after translating it? Or should these tasks be absorbed into the hourly charge for translating the document?

Oddly enough, translation clients (both translation agencies and direct clients) seem willing to pay a higher per-word rate than the hourly rate that the per-word rate translates into. For example, many experienced translators can produce about 500 finished (translated and proofread) words per hour. At a rate of

15 cents per word, that would translate into an hourly rate of $75, which is much higher than most agencies are likely to pay.

1.9 Professional associations for translators and interpreters

Professional associations are an excellent resource for both beginning and experienced translators and interpreters. At the international, national and local levels, professional associations allow you to network with colleagues, pursue continuing education workshops and attend conferences related to the field. They also improve your credibility as a linguist. As one agency manager comments, "If a person is a member of a professional association, it shows that he or she has a network of colleagues to draw on and is willing to invest some time and money in the profession." Following is an overview of professional associations for translators and interpreters.

1.9.1 American Translators Association

The American Translators Association http://atanet.org is the largest professional association for language professionals in the U.S., and offers membership to both individual linguists and translation companies; at this writing it has over 11,000 members. The Association also includes various language or specialization-specific divisions that members can choose to join. Benefits for ATA members include a listing in the ATA online directory, a subscription to the monthly *ATA Chronicle*, reduced rates to attend ATA conferences and seminars, and various professional benefits such as credit card acceptance, credit union membership and professional liability insurance. The ATA holds a large annual conference each fall and administers its own certification exams, which are probably the most widely recognized translation credential in the U.S. As of 2011, individual membership in the ATA costs $160 per year.

1.9.2 National Association of Judiciary Interpreters and Translators

The National Association of Judiciary Interpreters and Translators http://najit.org is a professional association for court interpreters and legal translators. NAJIT holds an annual conference, publishes the newsletter *Proteus*, and advocates for positive changes in the court interpreting and legal translation professions. NAJIT's website also includes a helpful list of Frequently Asked Questions (FAQ) about court interpreting. 2011 individual dues are $140 per year.

1.9.3 American Literary Translators Association

The American Literary Translators Association http://literarytranslators.org is dedicated to serving literary translators and "enhancing the status and quality of literary translation." Members receive a variety of publications about literary translation, such as *Translation Review* and ALTA *Guides to Literary Translation*, and ALTA also holds an annual conference on literary translation. 2011 individual dues are $80 per year.

1.9.4 Fédération Internationale des Traducteurs

The Federation International des Traducteurs http://fit-ift.org is an "association of associations" for translators, which gathers more than 100 associations for language professionals from all over the world. FIT does not accept individual translators as members, but does hold congresses that are open to translators and interpreters throughout the world. The 2011 FIT Congress will be held in San Francisco, CA in August.

1.9.5 International Association of Conference Interpreters

Membership in AIIC http://aiic.net is open only to experienced conference interpreters who have worked a minimum of

150 days in a conference setting. New members must be sponsored by three active AIIC members who have been in the association for at least five years. The AIIC website contains many helpful articles and links for aspiring and experienced interpreters.

1.10 Professional associations outside the U.S.

If you are based in the U.S., you may want to consider joining a professional association for translators and interpreters in your non-English language country. Following is some basic information about professional associations outside the U.S.

- Australian Institute of Translators and Interpreters: http://www.ausit.org

- Universitas (Austria): http://universitas.org

- Belgian Chamber of Translators, Interpreters and Philologists: http://www.cbtip-bkvtf.org

- ABRATES (Brazil): http://www.abrates.com.br

- Danish Association of State-Authorized Translators and Interpreters (DT): http://www.dtfb.dk

- Translatørforeningen (Denmark): http://www.translatorforeningen.dk

- Finnish Association of Translators and Interpreters: http://www.sktl.fi

- Panhellenic Association of Translators (Greece): http://www.pem.gr

- Irish Translators and Interpreters Association: http://www.translatorsassociation.ie

- Italian Translators Association: http://www.aiti.org

- Netherlands Society of Interpreters and Translators:
  http://www.ngtv.nl

- Romanian Translators Association:
  http://www.atr.org.ro

- Union of Translators of Russia:
  http://www.translators-union.ru

- ASETRAD (Spain): http://www.asetrad.org

- Swedish Translators Association: http://www.sfoe.se

- Swiss Association of Translators, Terminologists and Interpreters: http://www.astti.ch

- Institute of Translation and Interpreting (UK):
  http://www.iti.org.uk

- Mexican Translators Association: http://www.omt.org.mx

- Canadian Translators, Terminologists and Interpreters Council: http://www.cttic.org

- Argentina Association of Translators and Interpreters:
  http://www.aati.org.ar

- Association of Translators and Interpreters of Chile:
  http://www.cotich.cl

- Costa Rica Association of Professional Translators and Interpreters: http://www.acotip.org

- Association of Translators and Interpreters of Ecuador:
  http://www.atiec.org

- Association of Translators and Interpreters of Guatemala:
  http://www.agitguatemala.org

- Peruvian Association of Professional Translators:
  http://www.atpp.org.pe

- Panama Association of Translators and Interpreters:
  http://www.aptipanama.com

- Association of State Translators of Uruguay:
  http://www.colegiotraductores.org.uy

- Association of Translators and Interpreters of Venezuela:
  http://www.conalti.org

- Egyptian Translators Association: http://www.egyta.com

- South African Translators Institute:
  http://translators.org.za

- Translators Association of China:
  http://www.tac-online.org.cn

- Indian Translators Association: http://www.itaindia.org

- Japan Association of Translators: http://jat.org

- Iraqi Translators Association:
  http://www.irtrans.org

- New Zealand Society of Translators and Interpreters:
  http://www.nzsti.org

1.11 Certification for translators

For better or worse, you don't have to have any type of certification to call yourself a translator or interpreter in the United States. The American Translators Association offers translator certification exams and court interpreters can be certified at the state or federal level but these exams apply only to certain language combinations.

At present, the ATA exam is a three-hour written exam in which you translate two passages of 225-275 words each. ATA is starting to offer some computerized exam sittings but most are still hand written. One exam passage is on a general topic and everyone must translate the general passage. For the second passage, candidates have a choice between science/technology/medicine or law/business/finance. In order to pass the exam, you must pass both passages.

Before you invest in the $300 (as of 2011) registration fee for the ATA exam, it's a good idea to take a practice test. Practice tests are available to ATA members for $50 per passage, and you receive your graded passage back with comments. When you take the actual exam, you do not receive your graded exam back (only the results) unless you pay an additional review fee of $250. Given that the overall pass rate on the ATA exams is below 20%, it's well worth your while to spend $50 or $100 on trying one or two practice exam passages before you register for the actual exam.

The value of certification depends on your professional goals and the areas in which you work. Non-certified English<>Spanish court interpreters may have a hard time finding work and according to the most recent ATA compensation survey, certified translators earn about $6,000 per year more than their non-certified colleagues. However, there are plenty of non-certified translators and interpreters who earn a high income and don't feel a need to become certified. Before you decide to pursue certification, make sure that being certified will help you meet a specific professional goal. For example if you are new in the industry or trying to break into a new market, certification can be a big plus.

Following is an overview of the main certifying organizations for translators and interpreters in the United States. If you work in a language combination that doesn't involve English, see the previous section of a list of professional associations for translators and interpreters outside the U.S.

1.11.1 American Translators Association

The American Translators Association http://atanet.org offers *certification* (formerly called *accreditation*) to translators in the following language pairs as of 2011:

- Arabic into English

- English into Chinese

- Croatian into English, English into Croatian

- Danish into English

- English into Dutch

- English into Finnish

- French into English, English into French

- German into English, English into German

- English into Hungarian

- English into Italian

- Japanese into English, English into Japanese

- English into Polish

- Portuguese into English, English into Portuguese (test not offered in 2011)

- Russian into English, English into Russian

- Spanish into English, English into Spanish

- English into Ukrainian

Candidates for the ATA certification exam must fulfill an education and experience requirement before being allowed to sit for the exam. In order to take the ATA exam (not the practice exam), you must meet one of the following requirements:

- Certification or accreditation by an organization that is a member of the Fédération Internationale des Traducteurs.

- A degree or certificate from an approved Translation and Interpreting program (see ATA website for list of approved programs) or a Master's degree, PhD or equivalent degree in any field.

- A Bachelor's degree and two years' experience working as a translator or interpreter (see ATA website for how to demonstrate your work experience).

- Less than a Bachelor's degree and five years' experience working as a translator or interpreter (see ATA website for how to demonstrate your work experience).

1.11.2 Federal Court Interpreter Certification Examination Program

The Federal Court Interpreter Certification Examination Program http://cps.ca.gov/fcice-spanish/index.asp is perhaps the most widely recognized credential for interpreters in the United States. Passing this examination, most commonly offered in Spanish↔English but also in Navajo↔English and Haitian Creole↔English, earns you the designation *Federally Certified Court Interpreter*. The examination is rigorous, necessitating that the candidate maintain simultaneous interpreting speeds of up to 160 words per minute, and retain passages of up to 50 words in length for consecutive interpreting. FCICE candidates must first pass a written test with a score of at least 75%, and are then invited to take the oral portion of the exam, on which a score of 80% is considered passing. At present, the oral portion consists of a sight translation, simultaneous interpretation and mock cross-examination, involving both consecutive and simultaneous interpretation. The exam is offered on specific dates in specific locations specified on the program's website, so if you don't live near one of these cities, you'll have to travel there in order to take the exam.

A self-assessment of readiness to take the FCICE exam is included on the program website, and numerous preparation courses have sprung up in order to meet the growing demand especially for Spanish↔English court interpreters in certain areas of the United States. Other than the FCICE site itself, an excellent resource is Acebo, a language resources company run by highly qualified interpreter trainers. The Acebo website http://acebo.com has a section with "Tips for the Federal Exam," and also sells preparation materials for interpreting exams, the most popular of which are *The Interpreter's Edge* and *The Interpreter's Edge Turbo Supplement*.

1.11.3 State court interpreter certification

Court interpreter certification at the state level is much less standardized than at the federal level. Some states such as Washington, New Jersey, California and Colorado have active programs to certify court interpreters of Spanish and other languages as well, and strongly suggest that courts use only certified interpreters. Other states are moving toward this type of model, while still others have no certification procedures at all. The best source of information on what's available in your state is The Consortium for Language Access in the Courts http://www.ncsconline.org. The Consortium has developed interpreter certification tests in Modern Standard Arabic, Egyptian Colloquial Arabic, Cantonese, Bosnian/Serbian/Croatian, French, Haitian Creole, Hmong, Ilocano, Korean, Laotian, Mandarin, Polish, Portuguese, Russian, Somali, Spanish, Turkish and Vietnamese (some of these languages have a full examination while others have an abbreviated or partial one). Examinations for Chuukese, Hindi, Marshallese and Panjabi are in development. As of this writing, the 2011 exam schedule is not posted on the NCLAC website but you can check back for more information

1.12 Resources

- The American Translators Association: http://www.atanet.org

- The American Literary Translators Association: http://www.literarytranslators.org

- The National Association of Judiciary Interpreters and Translators: http://www.najit.org

- The International Association of Conference Interpreters: http://www.aiic.net

- Acebo (training materials for interpreters): http://www.acebo.com

- *Translator Self-Training* (series of books by Morry Sofer, available for numerous language combinations): http://www.amazon.com

- *The Entrepreneurial Linguist* by Judy and Dagmar Jenner: http://www.entrepreneuriallinguist.com

- *The Prosperous Translator* by Chris Durban: http://www.prosperoustranslator.com

- Translation Journal: http://translationjournal.net

- Translatortips: http://translatortips.com

- New York University's Professional Certificate in Translation program: http://scps.nyu.edu

- University of Chicago's Translation Studies Certificate program: http://grahamschool.uchicago.edu

- Monterey Institute of International Studies: http://www.miis.edu

- Kent State University Institute of Applied Linguistics: http://appling.kent.edu

2 Launching your freelance translation business

2.1 The startup phase

Succeeding as a freelance translator partially depends on whether you can push through your startup phase into full-time work and profitability. Many factors will affect the length of your startup phase, but in general it's good to plan on at least six months to a year if you want to freelance full time. If you have existing contacts in the industry, a degree in translation or interpreting or a degree in a specialized area that is in demand in the industry, and you market yourself aggressively, you may be working full time within a few months.

At first, this may seem like a daunting idea. But just like someone who opens a consulting firm or a furniture store, you are starting a business, and your startup expenses will be relatively low by comparison. The keys to a successful startup phase are assertive marketing, careful financial planning and realistic expectations. The main startup expense of your freelance business will be your time, so you will need to plan financially for a period of spotty income. However, if you execute the startup phase correctly, you will then have a profitable, flexible and intellectually stimulating business for as long as you want to keep running it.

2.2 Ways to start

Fortunately, the direct costs associated with starting a translation business are low: a reliable computer, office software and maybe a translation environment tool, a high-speed internet connection and a business phone are about all you need to get going. The real cost of starting a freelance translation business is time. If you only have five hours per week in which to start your business, you may be able to make some extra income but you won't be working full time in three months. On the other hand, if you devote yourself full time to starting your business, you will need to plan for how you will support yourself until you have a steady stream of work. Here are some ideas on ways to start your business:

Start slowly. While continuing to work another full time job, devote five to 10 hours per week to starting your translation business. Look for clients who have projects that are small and that do not have to be completed on a rush basis. These might include translating official documents such as birth certificates and school transcripts for individuals, legal aid agencies, consulates or immigration attorneys; or working with translation companies in your area that need someone to handle small projects. This situation works best if your current job allows you to slowly cut back your schedule as your translation work expands.

Work a part time job and freelance. Working part time can be an excellent way to pay your living expenses while you start your translation business. Such work might include teaching foreign language courses, working at a library or book store or doing editing or transcription work in your native language. One good option is to find part time work that you can do from home on a freelance basis (editing, transcription, copywriting, etc.) so that you are also available to take on translation work as it comes in.

Start full time. If you can afford it, devoting all of your work time to starting your freelance business is often the quickest way to get going. You should count on at least six months to a year of irregular work, so you will need either a substantial savings cushion, another means of support such as a spouse's or partner's income, or the willingness to take out a loan to support yourself.

2.3 The startup checklist

The length of your startup phase will vary depending on your language pair(s), specializations, flexibility and previous experience in the translation industry. The types of clients you'll be working with will also change as your business grows, a topic that will be addressed later in this book. Most beginning translators work with translation agencies, although some beginning freelancers with previous translation experience may want to work with direct clients. Following is a checklist of some tasks that you will need to complete during your first year in business. These are in roughly chronological order; some tasks may not apply to you at all, while you may need to repeat others several times in order to get your business up and running.

- Phase 1: Research and Preparation
    - Learn about the translation industry. Visit the website of your national, regional and/or local translators associations. Contact three to five working translators to ask about their experience in the industry and their suggestions for a beginning freelancer.
    - Research the competition. Look at the online profiles and websites of translators working in your language combinations; see what specializations and services they offer and whether they publish their rates.
    - Write your translation-targeted resumé and cover letter and make sure they are error-free.
    - Research the types of clients you would like to work with. Visit some translation agencies' websites and click on "Careers," "Freelancers," "Employment" or other likely links to see if the agency is accepting applications and what information they ask for. If you find any translation agencies that work primarily or only in your language pair, make a note of them. If you would like to work with direct clients, think about whether you will need additional specialists, such as an editor, to work with you.

- Get your home office up to speed. Make sure that you have at least one powerful and reliable computer with a reliable backup system and preferably a backup computer, and that your computer software is up to date. Consider whether you need a dedicated business phone line and faxing capabilities.

- Have translation-specific business cards printed and always (always!) have some with you.

- Set your range of rates.

- Phase 2: Initial contacts

    - If you have any existing contacts either in the translation industry or with direct clients who might need your services, contact them and let them know that you have launched your freelance business.

    - If you plan on working with translation agencies, set a schedule that will allow you to contact 300-500 potential clients during your first year in business, assuming that you would like to be working full time in six months to a year. The membership directories of translators associations in your source and target language countries are excellent sources of contacts, but always contact an agency by going to its website and following the application process listed there.

    - Contact any potential clients in your local area and ask for an informational interview.

    - Consider whether you need additional marketing materials such as a website, brochures or marketing postcards.

    - Actively network with other translators: get involved in your local translators association, in a Division of the American Translators Association, online translation portals and/or in non-translation specific associations such as local freelancers' groups, your local World Trade Center or chamber of commerce.

- Phase 3: Follow-up and growth

    - Keep a log of all of the business contacts you make (this can be electronic, on paper, or any method that works well for you) and any contacts that send you a positive response, even if it's just "thanks for your application, we'll contact you if we need you." Every two to three months, contact these people again and let them know what new projects you have been working on, and that you are still interested in working with them if they need you.

    - If you have time, send a handwritten thank you note with a business card in it to everyone who responds positively to your initial contact. In the sea of e-mails that these recruiters and project managers receive, your card will stand out and show that you are eager to work with that company.

    - When you start to get some work, ask your clients for feedback on whether you met their expectations and whether you could do anything better to meet their needs in the future. If the client is happy with your work, ask for a testimonial to share with your prospective clients.

2.4 Preparing for your job search

Whether you're just starting out as a translator or moving from in-house to freelance work, finding your first clients is one of the biggest challenges you'll face. For most beginning translators, it will be hard to find well-paying work unless you have either a degree in translation or some translation experience. If you have both excellent language skills and work experience in a technical field, for example if you are a doctor and bilingual in Russian, it may be worth sending off your resumé even without translation experience. For the rest of us, it's important to compose a file of samples and references before applying to agencies or direct clients. Here are some ways to go about beefing up your resumé if you're starting from zero.

2.4.1 The basics of writing a translation resumé

Having a translation-targeted resumé is your most crucial first step in starting your job search. Since some translation agencies will look *only* at your resumé, it's especially important to have a strong one, as your cover letter may never be seen by the person responsible for delegating projects. If you are e-mailing your resumé, you should send it in either Microsoft Word format or as a PDF. Whatever the format of your resumé, it is absolutely imperative that it is well written and contains *no errors* in grammar or spelling. Remember, you are applying for language work— why would a potential client trust this work to someone whose own application materials don't show evidence of good language practices? Let's look at some important features of a well-written translator resumé.

2.4.2 A new resumé for a new career

The number one thing your resumé needs to do is convince a potential client to take a chance on you instead of giving the job to a more experienced linguist. Many beginning translators fail from the get-go because they use the same resumé that they've been sending out to look for a job in banking, health care, teaching or sales, wrongly assuming that they have nothing to write about their qualifications as a translator. If you are not familiar with writing a resumé, or with writing one for the U.S., large online job search sites such as Monster.com `http://monster.com` have extensive "career search help" sections that can help you get started and learn how to format your resumé. Even if you are familiar with how to write a strong resumé, spend some time on the Web looking at how other translators present themselves; online translation portals such as Translators Café `http://translatorscafe.com` and ProZ.com `http://proz.com` are good places to start.

The first step in the resumé reinvention process is to think about and research what your potential clients are looking for in a translator. Obviously they want someone who knows at least two languages, but on top of that, think about your prospective clients' needs and wants. For example, translators need to be able to work independently on tight deadlines without the oversight of a boss. Translators work on computers almost all the time, and need to know how to use computers efficiently. Translators also need excellent writing skills in their target language and excellent communications skills to work well with clients. Specialized translators need to know terminology in their areas of specialization. Some or all of these skills may be transferable from your current career. Therefore, it can be a good idea to start out your resumé-writing process by writing down the key career skills you've developed that will make you attractive to a new client.

2.4.3 The structure of your resumé

This section will focus mainly on writing a resumé for use in the U.S. However, it is a good idea to have resumés in both your source and target languages so that you can apply to translation agencies or direct clients in your non-native language countries. Make sure to follow good translation practice yourself and have the resumé in your non-native language proofread by a native speaker. Following are some factors to consider when preparing your resumé for use in the U.S. or abroad.

- A resumé for use in the U.S. is quite streamlined compared to what's expected in many other countries. It is generally only one page long, two pages at most, and does not include much personal information other than your name and contact information, including address, telephone number and email address. If you are going to be posting your resumé on the Internet, consider removing your physical address from that version of your resumé. Identity theft from online job applications is a risk, so never include information such as your Social Security Number on your online information. A U.S. resumé can be organized either chronologically (usually starting with your current job and going in reverse), or functionally (using categories such as **Professional Qualifications, Skills Summary** etc.). A resumé for the U.S. is *always* typeset (not handwritten), and uses lots of active verbs, promoting the person's accomplishments: "established," "created," "managed," etc. A U.S. resumé, unlike resumés for some other countries, also tends to emphasize what the prospective employer will gain from hiring the candidate rather than what the candidate would like to gain from the employer.

- A resumé for use in Europe contains much more personal information. It is common to list your date and place of birth, citizenship(s), marital status, and sometimes even number of children. A scanned photograph is also sometimes included. This type of information should *never* be included on your U.S. resumé since it is actually illegal for employers to ask for it in most cases. If you send a European resumé through the mail, it is sometimes seen as a "plus" to send a handwritten resumé and cover letter. Many European employers feel that a handwritten resumé or cover letter lets them evaluate your language skills and it may also be submitted for an analysis of your personal traits as revealed through your handwriting. On a European resumé, "chronological order" normally means reverse chronological order, so you would start with your first job and end with the one you have now. European resumés also tend to be less promotional in nature, and use more passive and descriptive language such as "responsibilities included..."

- An Asian resumé is much more comprehensive than a U.S. or even a European one. For example, while on a U.S. resumé you would seldom include levels of education below college or professional school unless you didn't attend these, on a resumé to be sent to Japan or China your **Education** section might include every school you attended starting with kindergarten, which would reveal insights into your family's socioeconomic status.

2.4.4 Your name

The first item on your resumé will be your name. Give some thought to the name you use professionally, especially because you will be dealing with multilingual and multicultural work environments:

- You may want to clarify your gender. In your source language culture, your name may be gender indeterminate, making it awkward when potential clients don't know how to address you. If you want, you can solve this problem up front by identifying yourself somewhere on your application materials as "Fouad Tarkari (Mr.)" or "Ms. Poonam Prakash." Likewise, U.S.-based translators may want to do this when sending materials to their source language countries.

- Choose one name and spelling, and use it consistently. Especially if your name involves any transliteration, pick one version and stick to it. Going by different names can also present payment problems when the agency writes a check or tries to complete a wire transfer under a different spelling of your name.

2.4.5 Your tag line

A tag line that summarizes what you do, such as "English to Japanese financial translator," "Registered Nurse and French to English Translator" or "ATA-Certified Danish to English translator" is a great way to allow potential clients to quickly screen your resumé. At a minimum, always prominently state your language pairs immediately below or next to your name. Stick to translating into your native language only, unless you consider yourself as having two native languages.

A line with your specializations can also be helpful. For example your first tag line could be "German to English translator" and your second could be "Specializing in medical and pharmaceutical translations," or "Specializations: legal, financial and marketing translations." All of this "sound bite" information will allow prospective clients to quickly determine if they have a need for your services.

2.4.6 Your contact information

You need to include some type of contact information on your resumé, but how much to include is up to you. Some translators include their mailing address and some don't, some include just a general geographical location such as "Utah, USA" or "New York metro area." Before you send out resumés, make sure that you have a dedicated business phone number to include. Some translators choose to make their cell phone the business phone line, some have a separate land line installed and some use a custom ring number that runs over their regular home phone line. You should also include your e-mail address, and make sure that it is a professional one. The best e-mail address, because it is the most permanent, is one that is associated with a domain name that you own, for example yourname@yourdomain.com. Because of issues with reliability and your clients' spam blockers, you should avoid using a free webmail address unless it is from a reputable provider. If you will be dealing with clients in various time zones and countries, it can also be helpful to include your time zone, which is normally expressed as a number of hours ahead of or behind Greenwich Mean Time, i.e. GMT+3, GMT-7, etc.

2.4.7 Your objective

If you are applying for freelance work, it is not usually necessary to list an objective on your resumé, since it is obvious that your goal is to find new freelance clients. The space that an objective takes up can be better used for other information.

2.4.8 Your summary of qualifications

This section, which goes below your name and contact information and might also be called a **Profile** section, is key to getting started as a translator. If the first item on your resumé is a detailed description of your ten years of work as a lab technician with no mention of language skills, clients may not even make it to the **Education** section to find out that you're actually bilingual in English and Japanese and interested in pharmaceutical translation; with a summary of qualifications you highlight this fact right away. A good way to research what qualifications your potential clients want is to read some translation agency websites; after all, you'll be delivering a good deal of the product that they're promising their clients. Including some of these desired characteristics is a good way to start your resumé on a positive note.

2.4.9 The body of the resumé

Next, you'll have to decide whether to structure your resumé functionally or chronologically. If the type of translation work you're seeking is somewhat related to your current work, you might opt for a chronological resumé. For example if you're currently a lawyer and would like to do legal translation, your resumé can be structured fairly traditionally. If you're breaking off on a completely new path, for example if you've worked as a tax preparer for five years and would like to do website translation, you may opt for a functional resumé, which in the most extreme examples doesn't even include your job titles or where you've worked, just summaries of your skills and experience.

When you're writing your first translation-targeted resumé, you should highlight any experience you have, both in the areas of language and subject matter. If you studied abroad in Mexico in 1975, include it. If you belong to a local translators association, include it. If you recently attended a conference on estate and will terminology, include it. If you just taught a French class for elementary school students, include it. Obviously you can't fabricate resumé details, but if you're planning to make translation your full-time or only job, it is fair to refer to yourself as a "self-employed freelance translator" (including your language pairs) and describe the work you are doing now. As your translation experience grows (and it will!), change the format of your resumé to reflect this.

2.4.10 The professional/related experience section

Here, you should list any translation or translation-related experience that you have. If you have done previous translation work even on a volunteer basis, you should include it right at the beginning of this section so that prospective clients will see it first. If you have no direct translation experience but you have some translation-related experience such as interpreting, teaching foreign language courses, writing or editing, make sure to highlight that as well.

If you are applying for freelance work, it is acceptable to have gaps in your employment history, and it may be better to omit jobs that are completely unrelated to translation than to include them. In addition, if you have a gap in your employment history because you took time off, whether to raise children, take care of aging relatives or follow a spouse's job relocation, don't feel the need to explain it unless a client asks. In general, clients are much less concerned about a freelancer's employment gaps than they would be about a full-time employee's.

In your professional/related experience section, try also to highlight transferable skills. If you have ever been successfully self-employed, or worked in a job that involved tight deadlines or done work that involved writing or editing, emphasize that experience. In addition, if any of your jobs required you to learn terminology associated with a specialized field (medicine, banking, law, computer hardware/software, automotive, pharmaceuticals, aerospace, marketing, etc.) make sure to include that.

If you are a recent college graduate with no employment history, highlight your language and cultural experience as well as any internships or volunteer work that you've done. In general, young translators need to show that they are trustworthy and reliable despite their lack of employment history.

2.4.11 The education section

You should include some information about your education, at least any undergraduate and graduate degrees you have earned. At a minimum, you should list the degree you earned, the name of the college or university, the location of the college or university and your major or specialization. You do not have to include the year you graduated if you do not want prospective clients to know your approximate age. If you took courses toward a degree but did not complete the program, you can include that information as long as you specify "20 credits toward Master of Arts in Art History" or something similar. If you studied abroad or participated in a special program in which you used your foreign language skills, make sure to include that.

2.4.12 The professional development and memberships section

Professional association memberships are a real boost to your resumé. Membership in a professional association shows that you have a network of colleagues and are willing to invest some time and money in your profession. You can include a short section with a bulleted list, such as "Member, American Translators Association" or "Member, New York Circle of Translators," and also list any translation-related conferences, workshops or courses that you have participated in.

2.4.13 The computer skills and equipment section

If you need to fill some space on your resumé and you have specialized computer skills, this is a good section to include. For example, if you already know how to use translation-specific software, you will stand out from the pool of beginner translators. If you are proficient in the use of software for desktop publishing or web design, this is also an asset.

2.4.14 The interests and activities section

This is another section that you can include or omit depending on your preferences and how much room you have on your resumé. Listing your interests and activities is certainly not necessary, but it serves a few purposes. First, in an industry where business is conducted almost entirely by e-mail and phone contact, this type of section helps clients get to know you a bit as a person. Also, you never know when a client will have an unusual translation that requires someone who knows the terminology of a particular activity, such as sailing, rock climbing, sign language or photography.

2.4.15 What about a cover letter?

Since most freelance translation work is conducted over the Internet, a formal cover letter really isn't necessary or even appropriate for most translators. The exception would be if you are interested in doing direct client work, in which case you might be sending your materials through the mail or by fax instead of over the Web. Most of the time, you will either send a short e-mail cover letter, or include a paragraph or two in the "Additional Information" field of a translation agency's online application.

Your e-mail cover letter should be short and to the point. Keep in mind that many translation agencies receive several thousand unsolicited translator applications per year, and it's unlikely that whoever receives your e-mail will take the time to read a long message. So, pare down your message to the essentials. Following are a few tips to help you craft an effective e-mail cover letter:

- Address the prospective client by name. Use "Dear Mr./Ms." if you have the name of a direct contact person, or "To the attention of ABC Translations" if you don't. Double, triple, quadruple-check to make sure that you spell the name of the company or individual correctly.

- Use an honest and descriptive subject line, such as "English to Japanese freelance translator" or "Inquiry from English to German freelancer." Using "trick" subject lines will only anger your potential client and waste their time.

- Hit the important points as quickly as possible: "I am a freelance English to Italian translator specializing in subtitling and I would like to offer my freelance services to you," or "I am responding to your posting for French to English financial translators" or something equally straightforward.

- If you have a degree in translation, a translation certificate or certification, mention it in the first paragraph.

- If you are a beginner, don't lie about your experience but don't call attention to it either. Your potential clients will see that you've only been freelancing for a short time; let them be the judge of whether you can do the work that they need.

- In general, do not discuss rates in your initial contact unless you're responding to a posting that requires your rate information. Sell the client on your quality before you talk about money.

- Proofread, proofread, proofread! Remember, you are applying for *language work*. Even a single error in your cover letter is unacceptable. Look out especially for "wrong word" errors such as it's/its, your/you're etc.

- Resist the urge to tell your life story. Stick to your professional qualifications and save your personal story for when you get to know the client.

- Keep your e-mail cover letter brief. Three or four paragraphs of three or four sentences each is probably the maximum that a prospective client will read.

- Always include your full contact information and time zone so that the prospective client can contact you. Close your e-mail with some information about your preferred next step, such as "Thank you for your time and consideration, please feel free to let me know if you need any additional information" or "Thank you for taking the time to review my application, I will contact you to follow up within the next few weeks."

2.5 Finding your first clients: agencies

If you're starting out by applying to translation agencies, remember to play by their rules in order to maximize your chances of getting work. Most agencies have a translator application form on their websites; the "Contact Us," "Freelancers" or "Opportunities" sections of agency websites are good places to look for these. Although it feels impersonal to apply for work this way, resist the urge to distinguish yourself by sending in a paper resumé if the agency requests an electronic one; what seems to you like a personal touch will only create more work for your potential client and may get your application materials tossed without a second look. Most agencies prefer not to be contacted by phone unless you are applying for a specific position that they've advertised. If the online application form includes a "Comments" field, this is the place to ask for an in-person meeting or introduce yourself as a new translator in the area. For translation agencies in the United States, the website of the American Translators Association http://atanet.org is a good place to find an agency's web address, and the agency's profile on the ATA website may also indicate if it is currently accepting applications from new translators.

2.5.1 Finding your first clients: direct clients

Looking for work with direct clients has some positive and negative points for a beginning translator. As a newcomer to the profession, it can be helpful to have some of the safety nets that a translation agency offers. However, direct clients, especially those located in areas where there are not many translators to choose from, may be more likely than a translation agency to take a chance on an inexperienced translator. Whereas a translation agency has a wide range of translators to choose from with no geographic restrictions, a direct client who wants to work with someone local has a bigger incentive to work with someone new.

If you'd like to work with direct clients, any large businesses, hospitals or school systems in your area are worth contacting, even if they don't have obvious international ties. International chambers of commerce are excellent sources of potential clients since you can be sure that their members have some potential need for your services. Joining one of these organizations is also an excellent way to network with potential clients. Following is a list of the websites for some international chambers of commerce:

- New York chapter of the French-American Chamber of Commerce http://faccnyc.org

- New York chapter of the German-American Chamber of Commerce http://gaccny.com

- Chicago chapter of the Italian-American Chamber of Commerce http://italianchamber.us

- United States-Mexico Chamber of Commerce http://usmcoc.org

- Korean Chamber of Commerce and Industry in the U.S. http://kocham.org

- Japanese-American Chamber of Commerce, Silicon Valley http://jaccsv.com

- Polish-American Chamber of Commerce of Illinois http://polishamericanbusiness.com

- Swedish-American Chamber of Commerce http://sacc-usa.org

- Greek-American Chamber of Commerce http://greekamericanchamber.org

- Danish-American Chamber of Commerce in New York http://daccny.com

- Spain-US Chamber of Commerce http://spainuscc.org

- Vietnamese-American Chamber of Commerce, Minnesota http://vietnamesechamber.com

- Brazilian-American Chamber of Commerce of Florida http://brazilchamber.org

- Dutch-American Chamber of Commerce of Seattle http://daccseattle.com

- Asian Chamber of Commerce of Arizona http://asianchamber.org

2.5.2 Finding your first clients: general tips

Whatever route you'd like to take toward finding your first clients and building up your business, following are some tips that are applicable to almost every freelance translator's startup phase:

Be realistic. If you've never worked as a translator or interpreter before, starting out by contacting the United Nations or accepting a 20,000 word document on nuclear power plant safety procedures probably isn't the best way to start. Look for projects that you can do a great job on, and then use those projects to build up your business. Realize that it could easily take a year to build up a base of regular clients.

Network, network, network. Although most translators are introverts by nature, many job search experts identify networking as the most powerful job search strategy, and starting your translation business is no exception. Talk about your business with everyone you know, and give them a business card; strike up a conversation with the receptionist in every office you wait in, and leave a business card. Volunteer for your local translators association and get to know the experienced translators in your language pair; prepare an "elevator speech" (a few sentences that summarize what you do) and be ready to give it to anyone who asks you about your job!

Think locally. Especially if you present yourself better in person than on paper, start out by asking for in-person meetings with every translation or interpreting agency in your local area. By asking for a meeting to learn more about the potential client and talk about how you might fit in, you'll both benefit from the interaction. Don't be dissuaded if local clients "have no work in your language combinations right now." By asking for an in-person meeting, you'll position yourself to step in when their needs change.

Blanket the field. One of the biggest mistakes made by beginning translators and interpreters is to assume that you'll be working full-time after sending out five or ten inquiries. On the contrary, you should expect no more than a one percent return rate on your cold-contacting efforts to agencies; your return rate on direct client marketing may be higher.

Join some associations. Membership in a professional association establishes your seriousness as a linguist and allows you to make contact with colleagues in your area. Even for established linguists, referrals from colleagues are an important source of work. If you're very resourceful and very lucky as a beginner, you may even find a colleague in your language combination who is willing to take you on as an assistant or send some extra work your way.

Keep in touch. Instead of just firing off e-mails or making phone calls and then waiting to hear back from your potential clients, keep a log of the person you talked to or e-mailed with and what his or her response was to your inquiry. As you get more experience, periodically contact these people to let them know that you're still interested and available. Let them know what types of projects you've been working on, and let them know that you would be happy to help them out with similar jobs.

2.6 Key questions to ask before the project starts

Landing your first few clients will be one of the most exciting experiences of your freelance career; after all of your hard work planning and preparing, the day will come when a client will offer you a real live paying translation job, and it's incredibly exciting. At the same time, it's important to keep a level head and realize that being offered the project doesn't mean that you just say "Yes," without even knowing what the work consists of. Sometimes, saying "No" can be a better decision for your career in the long run. It is critical to remember that it takes a lot of hard work to build a good reputation, and just one poorly done project to spoil that reputation.

Before accepting a project, ask yourself...

- *Am I comfortable with the subject matter?* Along with failing to investigate a potential client's trustworthiness, this is probably the biggest mistake made by beginning translators. If you don't know the difference between AC and DC power or what a solenoid is or how to change a spark plug, you'll be even more lost when trying to understand these items in one of your source languages. At the start, stick to material you feel very comfortable with. If you'd like to branch out into a more technical specialization, take some courses on the topic in your native language, and consider paying a translator who is experienced in that particular specialization to edit your work until you feel confident in your skills.

- *Can I finish this translation on time?* Tight deadlines are the reality of the modern business world, but you have to train yourself to recognize the difference between tight and impossible. 2,500 words due tomorrow is a tight deadline; 10,000 words due tomorrow is an impossible deadline. For a tight deadline, it's fair to charge a higher rate to make up for the fact that you have to work overtime; for an impossible deadline, the only course of action that will preserve the quality of your work is to say "No!"

- *Am I confident that this client will pay me?* If the client has a good track record of payment, the chances are that your money will come through. If the client is not an established business, it's up to you to judge and deal with the consequences. Just as you will be asking clients to take a chance on you as a new translator, you may need to take chances on your clients, but make sure to follow the steps previously discussed for investigating your clients before you work for them. Get full contact information and a written guarantee of payment before you start working.

- *Am I getting paid fairly for my work?* As a new translator, some of your prospective clients will be low paying, and this doesn't make them bad clients. Still, working for impossibly low rates devalues your own work and the work of other professional translators. If you agree to work for less than your usual rate, it should be for a good reason; for example the client is a non-profit organization, or the project is very large and has a flexible deadline.

Before accepting a project, ask the client some or all of the following questions. For small jobs from regular clients, you may not have to go through the entire list, and clients who have done their homework will often volunteer the answers to these questions before you ask.

- *What type of document is this?* What format is the document in (hard copy, handwritten, PDF, Word, Excel, HTML)? What is the subject matter?

- *How many words or pages is the document?*

- *What is the deadline?* Once you've asked this, make sure that you can make the deadline!

- *May I see a sample of the document before accepting the project?* This is always a good idea, and even if the material is highly confidential, the client should be able to e-mail or fax you something like the table of contents or the index. Seeing a sample helps you decide how long the translation will take— is it 20 pages of barely legible handwriting, or 20 pages of neatly typed copy? Does the document contain complex formatting that will have to be reproduced?

- *What will the translation be used for?* You need to know if the advertising text they're sending you is intended as a "for information only" document for their sales team, or to be published in a highly visible place. This is a critical question that many translators skip.

- *What format should I deliver the translation in?* You need to know what file format the client wants; in some rare cases the client may also want a faxed or mailed hard copy.

- *Should I reproduce the formatting of the source document?* In most cases, clients will want the translation to look as much as possible like the source document. Sometimes, they just want to know what the documents say, so the formatting doesn't matter.

- *Who will answer my questions about this translation?* Many beginning translators are afraid that asking questions will make them seem unequal to the task at hand. On the contrary, it's important that if you don't understand what a term means and can't find the answer in any of your usual resources, you don't just guess and hope that no one will notice. The client should tell you up front who will answer your questions and how to submit them.

- *My rate for this translation would be...* It is absolutely critical to settle the question of rates and payment terms before you accept any translation work. Make sure that you agree on a per word rate, and whether the rate is charged on the source or target word count; in some cases the rate will be hourly. Then, clarify what the client's payment terms are, and if the payment is not by check or direct deposit, clarify who is paying for costs such as wire transfer or credit card fees (normally the client pays their fees and you pay yours, but if you don't specify, some clients will deduct their bank fees from your payment). Some clients will tell you what they're willing to pay for a specific project, but most will ask what you'll charge. The first time this happens is incredibly anxiety-provoking, as you have only a few seconds to come up with a price that isn't insanely high or low. If you've done your own homework and made a rate sheet in advance, your nerves will be considerably calmer when you get to the point of discussing rates.

- *Please send me a purchase order, contract, or written confirmation of the guidelines for this project.* If the client is not a regular one, it's important to have some written evidence of your business agreement with them. Without this, it's your word against theirs as to what terms you agreed on.

2.7 Building up your business

Once you've landed your first few clients, marketing yourself becomes easier in the sense that you have something to tell new prospective clients about. In general, even a successful freelancer must spend at least ten percent of his or her time on marketing; for beginning translators this figure may increase to as much as 50 percent. Even when you have enough work, it's important to avoid financial peaks and valleys by marketing consistently.

It's also important to distinguish between marketing for more work and marketing for better work. After a few years in business, many competent translators are busy most of the time and do not need to market for more work. However, many of these people make the mistake of stopping their marketing efforts because they don't need more work. Here's where marketing can lead to better work as well; work that pays a higher per-word or hourly rate, work that is more interesting, more flexible, or more ongoing, thereby lowering the translator's administrative costs. In reality, being busy all the time is a powerful lever to use with prospective new clients, since you can honestly tell them that in order to work for them, you will need to raise your rates. Following are some ways to keep the checks rolling in once you've gotten your business off the ground initially.

Please the clients you've got. While marketing to new clients is a worthy and even necessary endeavor, it's far easier to keep your existing clients coming back. Regular clients who come to you are key to earning a high income. Doing a great job on every project, responding promptly to phone calls and e-mails, never missing a deadline, and being there for your clients in a pinch will help turn new clients into regulars.

Ask for referrals and testimonials. Preferably after you've just done an "above and beyond" job for a client, tactfully let him or her know that your business continues to grow thanks to referrals from satisfied clients. Better yet, ask your happy clients to put their experiences with you in writing to be posted on your website or included in future marketing materials.

Spread the word. As mentioned in the previous section, keep a log of all of the professional contacts you make, and periodically update these potential clients on your recent projects. The definition of "periodically" is up to you, but an appropriate frequency might be every one to three months; more often and your messages will grow annoying, less often and the agency representative may not remember you at all. It's possible to accomplish this task with a minimum of effort, by using a personalized e-mail such as this one:

Dear *Name of Contact*:

I am a freelance French to English translator registered with your agency, and I'd like to update you on some of my recent projects, in the event that you have similar needs in the future. In the past few months, I have worked on a variety of discovery documents for three different

```
intellectual property lawsuits, one of which involved a
patent infringement case. I've attached my updated resumé
for your consideration, and I look forward to the
opportunity of working together in the future.
```

Keep cold-contacting. Many experienced translators estimate that of their new clients, approximately half come from cold contacts and half from word of mouth referrals. Whatever your level of experience, cold-contacting is important. If you're actively trying to build your business, set a goal of making 25 or more cold-contacts each week. Don't fall into the trap of expecting too many responses from too few contacts.

Keep networking. In a profession largely populated by independent contractors, networking gets you in touch with your colleagues and clients, either in person or electronically. Attending events for linguists is a great way to meet colleagues who may be in a position to refer work to you. If you're after new clients, consider joining a professional association in your target industry, whether this is signmaking, auto parts manufacturing, health care or law. Other networking endeavors worth considering are speaking to high school and college students considering careers in translation, teaching a class on getting started as a freelance translator or interpreter or taking on an intern from a local high school or college foreign language program.

Get creative. Sending your resumé to potential clients is important, but other marketing tactics can be as effective or more effective, especially with direct translation buyers. Put together a file of work you've done for previous clients (with their permission) and send it to prospective clients, offering to do the same for them. Present a compelling reason for potential clients to spend money on translation, i.e. "Are Spanish-speaking Internet users finding you, or your competition?" "Few Americans who visit France speak French, yet few French hotels and restaurants have websites in English," etc. For a potential "big fish" client, show your work—translate the prospect's brochure or website homepage, lay it out attractively, and ask for a meeting to discuss how you can help the client's business grow by making it more international. Starting an e-newsletter of interest to your clients and prospective clients is another useful marketing tool, since you're providing your clients with information they want while keeping your name fresh in their minds.

Become an expert. Writing, speaking and consulting about translation and interpreting are great ways to get your name recognized. Contact professional journals in your specializations and offer to write an article about translation issues in their industry; write a booklet on *Tips for Translation Buyers* and send it to potential direct clients; speak at professional conferences; post an article on *How to Speak Successfully When Using an Interpreter* on your website—by now you've got one, right?

2.8 Starting a part-time translation business

Depending on your financial and time resources, it may not be possible for you to make freelance translation or interpreting your full-time job right away. Starting a part-time business is a viable option, as long as you are careful to run your business in a professional way. Part-time freelance businesses can be split into two categories; taking on part-time translation or interpreting work in addition to another job, and taking on part-time translation or interpreting work as your only job.

If you already have another job and cannot afford to quit, you may want to do translations at night or on weekends. In this situation, you have the advantage of taking as long as you need to build your business up to the point where it replaces your current income. However, you also have the challenge of staying productive and available to both your full-time employer and your translation clients. Translation is a fast-paced industry and clients who contact you may need a response to their inquiry immediately. If you'll be combining part-time translation work with a full-time job, it's important to choose your clients carefully so that you don't end up being unavailable when they need you. You may be better off taking work that doesn't have a tight deadline, rather than work that requires you to communicate with the translation client during your work day at your full-time job.

If you either don't want or don't need to work full time, starting a part-time freelance business as your only job is a possibility as well. Depending on your geographical location and language pairs, your main challenge may be limiting your workload to your desired schedule. In theory, the on-call nature of most freelance translation and interpreting work lends itself well to part-time work, since it seems like you should be able to simply accept or turn down projects as your schedule allows. In practice, this isn't always the case. When a regular client calls, it's hard to say "No," since you want to help them out and keep them as a client; when no one calls, you can't do much about it except increase your marketing efforts. Still, many freelancers can and do make a go of it part-time. Make sure to organize and run your business just as professionally as you would if you were working full time; your clients don't need to know that you work part-time unless they ask, so don't give them a reason to suspect that you're less committed than someone who works 40+ hours per week.

2.9 Business skills you'll need

As a freelance translator or interpreter, you'll be exchanging the freedom of self-employment for the responsibility of finding your own work, charging a fair rate for this work, making sure you get paid, tracking your own tax liabilities and many other tasks. In this section, we'll take a look at the non-language-related skills that make for a successful freelance business.

Marketing. Unless you have a pre-existing client base, for instance a former employer who is interested in hiring you as a freelancer, you'll need to be able to market yourself. "Marketing" sounds like a scary and imposing concept at first, but if you've ever applied for a job, you've marketed yourself. Working as a freelancer is just a matter of applying for work over and over again until you build up a group of regular clients. One of the most important elements of marketing yourself as a translator or interpreter is to determine your comfort level with various sales techniques such as cold-contacting, networking, and public speaking.

Communicating. People do business with people they like, so make excellent communications skills a priority. First, you have to actually *do* the communicating; answer all business-related phone calls and e-mails as soon as possible, always within the same business day and preferably within an hour, and change your voice mail message or e-mail auto-responder when you'll be out of the office for more than one business day. Be honest about your availability and don't promise miracles that you can't deliver. Second, you need to communicate in a way that is positive and professional. Answer the phone cheerfully; when someone contacts you for work, thank them for thinking of you. When you call a client back and they've already found another linguist, thank them for contacting you and ask them to keep you in mind in the future, rather than getting angry that they didn't wait for your response.

Accounting. Like marketing, this is a concept that sounds frightening if you've never done it before. Especially if you've always worked as a salaried employee, working as a freelancer will require much more record-keeping than you've done before. However, at its most basic level, accounting for a freelancer consists of keeping records of your income and expenses, something that is definitely within your grasp. As with communicating, the most important aspect of accounting is to do it; record every payment as soon as you receive it and save receipts for every business expense in order to minimize your headaches at tax time.

Using technology. For translators, the days of pen and paper work are long gone, and you'll need to know how to use, at a minimum, the Internet, e-mail and office software such as word processing and spreadsheet programs. Translation memory software can increase your productivity, and depending on your languages and specializations may be necessary to running a viable business, since some clients require it.

Billing and collections. As a freelance translator or interpreter, you'll usually be responsible for billing your clients yourself and following up if they can't or won't pay. For most freelancers, a simple system of sending invoices by e-mail is enough, and you can keep track of your invoices either with a spreadsheet or on paper. Billing is the fun part, because your work is completed, and the expectation is that you'll be paid on time. When this doesn't happen, the situation is less sweet. You'll need to learn how to deal with clients who won't pay because of disagreements about issues such as the quality and timeliness of your work, and with clients who can't pay because of their own poor financial situations.

Dealing with highs and lows. While this is more of a psychological skill than a business one, it's one of the most important assets that a freelancer needs. Whether you're translating, interpreting or selling cars, the market goes up... and the market comes down. Unless you're either very lucky, a great planner, or both, you'll have weeks where you want to unplug your phone so that clients will stop calling, and weeks where you feel like you'll never be called by a client again. To make it as a freelancer, you'll need to deal with these peaks and valleys on several fronts. Most practically, you'll need to develop a budgeting strategy that keeps you from spending too much when your checking account is full and going into debt when work is lean. Mentally, it's important to be productive even when you don't have much paying work, for instance by contacting new potential clients, updating your website or catching up on your accounting.

2.10 Setting up your office and your business

While it's possible to spend many thousands of dollars setting up an office for your freelance translation or interpreting business, it's equally possible to get going with a minimal investment while maintaining a professional image.

Having a dedicated place to work is important; it helps you stay focused and organized in your work environment, and at tax time it helps you claim office space as a business expense. Your office will probably be located in your home. Many translators and interpreters work from home for their entire careers, while some choose to rent office space once their businesses are on firm financial ground. Unless you have absolutely no space to set up an office in your home or have access to free office space outside your home, working from home is the most cost-effective option. As more libraries and places of business start to offer free or low-cost wireless Internet access, it's also an option to set up a very minimal office in your house, and do most of your work at another location on a laptop computer, although you may forgo the tax benefits of having a full-fledged home office.

In order to field inquiries from clients and research new client prospects, you'll need a land line or cell phone and a computer with e-mail and high-speed Internet. Translators and interpreters at all levels will want to invest in a variety of general and specialized dictionaries, both print and electronic. You'll also need office software on your computer. Translation memory (TM) software, also called CAT (computer-assisted translation) software is fast becoming a necessity as well, with prices ranging from free to several thousand dollars. A fax machine is convenient to have, but no longer a necessity as e-mailed PDF files are quickly replacing faxes.

For interpreters who spend most of their day on the road, a smartphone or wireless e-mail device is a must. More translators are also starting to use smartphones to check their e-mail but it's definitely possible to run a translation business without one.

2.10.1 Ergonomics

Translation is a great job, but working at a computer all day is not great for your physical health. To keep yourself comfortable and avoid repetitive strain injury, set your office up using ergonomic principles. As much as possible, your joints should be at right angles when you are sitting at your desk: position your computer monitor so that you look straight at its center rather than looking up or down; position your keyboard so that your elbows are at a 90 degree angle when you type; position your chair so that your knees form a 90 degree angle and your feet are flat on the floor. Avoid crossing your legs at your desk; if you find it comfortable, using a yoga ball or balance chair instead of a traditional office chair can help with this.

2.10.2 Organizing your business

When setting up your office, prepare for your business to grow! Scribbling down an invoice number, date and amount on a scrap of paper works fine if you're only sending out one invoice per month, but as your work volume increases, sloppy business practices will leave you with no business at all and at risk of a tax audit. Following are some tips for organizing your translating or interpreting business for maximum productivity.

Track billings and income. Log every invoice you issue, along with its amount and due date. Follow up with clients to make sure that they have received your invoices, and follow up with clients who are more than a few days late in paying you. When the client pays you, log the income using a spreadsheet, accounting software or on paper.

Know where your time goes. Using time-tracking software or a time tracking spreadsheet can help you determine how many billable hours you work each week or month and how much time you spend on non-billable activities.

Keep a "to do" list. Do not interrupt your work every time you think of a task that you need to do, such as sending out an invoice or checking with a client about a potential project. Instead, keep a to-do list and write these items down as you think of them. Then, give yourself a block of time to complete all of the to-do items at once.

Keep everything in one calendar. If you work from home, keep your business and personal appointments on one calendar so that you do not double-book.

2.11 Maximizing productivity

Flexibility is one of the main advantages of self-employment, and you don't want to take the "free" out of "freelance." However, many freelancers struggle to run a profitable business because they have poor time management skills. Managing your time effectively serves multiple purposes: you can work more and earn more money, you can get your work done in less time and have more time for your family or non-work interests and you can avoid the panic of constantly working in crunch mode to meet your deadlines.

- Strike a flexibility balance. Too little flexibility will leave you wondering why you're freelancing in the first place; too much and you won't be earning any money. For example, block out certain times during which you allow yourself to do non-work activities such as exercising, grocery shopping, going to medical appointments or getting together with friends. Limit non-work activities to these times only and consider yourself "at work" the rest of the time.

- Set quantifiable goals. Instead of amorphous targets such as "contact more new clients," draw up a list of concrete objectives that you must meet, such as "send out 20 resumés per week and follow up ten by phone."

- As much as possible, consider yourself "at work" when you're working from your home office. Close your office door. Don't answer your home phone unless you're expecting an important call and let your family know that you are not to be interrupted except in an emergency.

- Limit the time you spend reading and responding to e-mail. Unless you're expecting an important message, give yourself a set time to check e-mail, for example every hour on the hour for a maximum of ten minutes. A corollary to this is keeping separate personal and work e-mail accounts so that you are never tempted to spend work time on personal correspondence.

- Take breaks. Breaks help you stay productive and help decrease eye and hand strain. You'll probably find that you work best in certain increments of time, maybe one to two hours at a stretch. After that amount of time, get up from your computer and do something with a different physical and visual focus so that you can recharge. It's important to do this on a larger scale as well; do not allow yourself to perpetually work overtime. There is a lot of evidence to suggest that people who work about 35 hours per week are the most productive, and that people who consistently work 50 hours a week are no more productive than those who consistently work 40 hours a week.

- Keep often-used information at your fingertips. Write a checklist of questions you need to ask prospective clients (How many words/pages is your document? What format is it in? When you you need the translation for? What will you be using the translation for?). Keep an updated copy of your resumé ready to send out at all times. Have a list of clients that prospective clients can call for references. Consider posting some of this information on your website to that clients can refer to it whenever they want to.

2.12 For working parents

Freelance translation is a great career option for working moms and dads. Most freelancers work largely on their own schedule and rarely need to go in to a client's office; translation can also be very high-paying as compared with other work-from-home job possibilities.

If you have very young children and you want to be home with them, you may be able to either limit your freelance work to small, short-term projects or work at night and on weekends when your spouse or partner can watch the kids. If you have older children, you can probably tailor your schedule so that you can work during the day while your kids are at school, spend the afternoons with them and then put in a few hours in the evening while your kids do homework. Fortuitously, the slow periods of the business year (Christmas/New Year's, summer) often coincide with school vacations. Following are a few tips for freelancing moms and dads:

- Accept your limitations. Despite the advantages of freelancing, it just is not possible to be a full-time mom or dad and a full-time translator (and remain sane) without using outside child care. You need to either work part-time or arrange for child care.

- Look for clients whose schedule works with yours. If you are working part-time or you are the parent who is always on call for child-related emergencies, do not take on more work than you can realistically handle. Look for clients whose time zone works to your advantage. For example if you live in the U.S. and work with clients in Europe, you can work in the evenings and deliver your translations before your clients get to the office the next morning in their time zone.

- Maintain a highly professional image. Never talk on the phone when your clients can hear your children in the background. Clients don't need to know that you can't take on a project because your children are on vacation from school; just tell them that you are unavailable.

- Make peace with your choices. Working and raising children is an often wonderful, often tough and exhausting combination. Sometimes that combination will feel just right and other times you will feel like you are doing a poor job as both a parent and a translator. This balancing act is much easier if you feel confident about your choices, either to work more and spend less time with your kids or the other way around.

2.13 Resources

- The Wealthy Freelancer (blog and book):
  http://www.thewealthyfreelancer.com

- Get Rich Slowly: http://www.getrichslowly.org

- Freelance Switch (tips on getting started as a freelancer):
  http://www.freelanceswitch.com

- Second Act (for freelancers over 40):
  http://www.secondact.com

- Free Resumé Tips: http://www.free-resume-tips.com

- Resumé Writing Help: htp://www.resume-help.org

3 Your first year as a freelance translator

The first six to twelve months of your freelance career are probably the most critical; at the end of the first year, many freelancers make the decision either to stick with self-employment or to try another option. Many beginning freelancers make a few critical but avoidable mistakes: they don't have a plan for how to support themselves, they don't define their service offerings and what types of clients they're looking for, they expect too much return from too little marketing effort and thus they burn out before their business even has a chance to succeed. By creating a detailed plan of what you'll be doing during this "make or break" first year, you will give yourself the greatest possible chance of succeeding.

Here is a sample plan for a beginning freelancer; you can modify it to fit the specifics of your own business. This plan assumes that you have 10-20 hours a week to devote to your newly-launched freelance business. If you have less time, pick the activities that seem the most important for your goals. If you have more time, you can probably complete all of these activities in 4-6 months. This timeline assumes that your language skills are already at a level that allows you to translate successfully. If you need to improve your language skills, you should pursue that before you start your freelance business.

Stage 1
- Identify your language pair(s). Remember that in the U.S., the translation market is heavily geared toward translators who work into their native language.

- Identify the services you will offer: translation, interpreting, editing, proofreading, voiceovers, copywriting, audio/video transcription etc.

- Order a set of basic business cards with your name, your language pair(s) and your contact information. Don't make the cards too specific in case you decide to change your services or specializations.

- Research some professional associations, such as the American Translators Association, your local ATA chapter if there is one and any associations for freelance translators in your area. If it is in your budget, join these associations.

- Determine whether the American Translators Association offers translator certification for your language pair and whether you meet the eligibility requirements to take the test. Consider joining the ATA so you can order a practice test.

- Talk to at least two experienced freelance translators about their jobs. Ask them for their advice for your startup phase.

- *If time allows*: read the websites and blogs of as many freelance translators as you can find. Make notes about your observations. Note what services these translators offer, how they market themselves and what information they give about their rates.

Stage 2
- Start to determine what types of clients you would like to work for: agencies, direct clients or both.

- Write your translation-targeted resumé and cover letter, targeting these documents to the types of clients you would like to work with.

- Ask at least two experienced freelance translators to review your resumé and cover letter.

- Determine how you want to price your translation services. Research what translators in your language combination charge, and calculate how many hours per month you plan on working and what your monthly income goal is.

- Determine if you want to set up a professional website. If so, calculate your budget and whether you would like to design and create the site yourself or hire a web designer.

- If there is a translators association in your local area, attend at least one of their events.

- If you have joined ATA, sign up for and start reading the e-mail list of the division(s) that you would like to participate in.

- Start to research potential clients in your local area, whether these are agencies or direct clients.

- Set up an accounting system for your freelance business. Start saving receipts for any business expenses you incur.

- *If time allows*: find and read the back issues of as many translation association journals as you can. Many of these archives are online for free. Print and save any articles that you find especially helpful.

Stage 3

- Finalize your translation-targeted resumé and cover letter.

- If you are going to create a professional website, start work on it or select a web designer and have her/him start creating the site.

- If you have found some potential clients in your local area, e-mail or call them and ask for an informational interview, or offer to take one of their project managers out for coffee to learn more about their business.

- Send out at least 20 resumés per month to potential clients. Start keeping a log of all of your professional contacts.

- Research translation specializations and identify at least one specialization that you would like to pursue. Having a targeted specialization is one of the best ways to succeed quickly as a freelance translator.

- Talk to an accountant or tax planner about your tax situation. Decide how you will pay taxes on your freelance income (as a sole proprietor, LLC, S-Corp etc.). If necessary, start making estimated tax payments.

- Make sure that your computer skills are up to date. If not, enroll in some computer courses through your local library or community college.

- Determine whether you want/need to purchase translation memory software.

- Evaluate your current computer setup. Do you have a reliable and regular backup system? Do you have a backup computer? Do you have a place to work if your power or Internet access goes down?

- Evaluate your current office setup. Do you have a comfortable desk and chair? Is your office organized and pleasant to be in? Do you have a professional phone line or cell phone? Call your own office phone and listen to your message!

- *If time allows*: do some research on work productivity. Figure out what your most and least productive times of the day are. Set up a system that allows you to deal with e-mail as efficiently as possible.

Stage 4

- By this time, hopefully you will begin to have some paying translation work as your marketing and networking efforts pay off!

- Send out at least 20 resumés to potential clients and record these in the log that you started.

- When you receive a positive response from a potential client, send them a hand-written thank you note and enclose one or two of your business cards.

- Attend at least one in-person networking or professional development event for translators in your area.

- Start developing a glossary of subject-specific terms that you use frequently. You can do this using a simple spreadsheet or table, or you can investigate terminology management software.

- Set up your business to accept as many payment methods as possible. For example, you may want to accept checks in dollars, checks in non-US currencies, wire transfers and credit cards (possibly via PayPal). Don't miss out on a job because you can't figure out how to accept the client's money!

- Research pro bono translation opportunities in your language pair(s). These can be a good way to beef up your resumé while providing non-profit clients with a valuable service.

- Ask all of your clients for feedback on your translation services; when you receive very positive feedback, ask if you can include it as a testimonial on your website.

- Continue marketing steadily even as your work volume picks up–this is how you will avoid the "feast or famine" phenomenon as your business grows.

4 Marketing your freelance services

Marketing is probably the most overlooked aspect of running a freelance business; most beginning translators radically underestimate the amount of marketing that they will need to do in order to develop and maintain a viable base of regular clients. Once you've moved past the startup phase, it's important to maintain regular marketing efforts so that you can avoid the feast-or-famine phenomenon that plagues many freelancers, and so that you can raise your rates when you want or need to. In this chapter we'll look at marketing techniques that apply to translation agencies and to direct clients.

Remember to set realistic expectations for your marketing campaigns. If you are cold-contacting translation agencies, do not expect a return rate greater than 1-2%. If you would like to find four to eight agencies that will become regular clients, plan on applying to at least 300 to 400 agencies during your first year in business. This target is realistic if you break the work up into smaller chunks and market consistently; just make sure that you are not expecting too much return for too little marketing effort.

If you are targeting direct clients, your marketing work will probably involve fewer actual contacts, but more time spent on each of those contacts. For example, while it takes only a few minutes to apply to a translation agency, you might spend many hours researching a potential direct client before trying to sell them your services. You may also need to contact a direct client many times before you make a sale; as with marketing to translation agencies, just make sure that you aren't expecting too much success for too little effort.

4.1 Marketing to translation agencies

Most beginning translators work primarily with translation agencies. If you already have significant translation experience or your skills are in a high-demand language pair or specialization, marketing to direct clients right away may be worthwhile. But if your goal is to get your business up and running as quickly as possible, agencies are probably your best target. Once you have your application materials prepared, applying to agencies is a relatively quick and easy process, but it is important to have your application strategy in place before you start applying. Marketing to translation agencies is not difficult, because agencies are nearly always on the lookout for qualified translators. However, marketing to agencies is generally a high-volume process, so it's important to know where to find potential agency clients and how to increase your chances of being offered some work.

4.1.1 Finding agencies to apply to

You will probably want to apply to agencies in your own country and in your source language countries. Translation industry professional associations are good sources of agency contacts, but make sure to use these sources wisely. When you find an online directory of translation associations, never use the listings to contact agency owners or employees directly. Go to the websites of the agencies you would like to apply to and follow the instructions that are given there; usually agencies have either an online application form or a specific e-mail address to use for your resumé.

Translation industry client rating services are another good source of potential agency clients. For example, if you purchase a subscription to Payment Practices or a similar translation client rating service, you can use the site's search function to list just the agencies that have been highly rated by other translators. This is a good way to avoid applying to agencies with poor payment track records. Searching for highly-rated agencies in a specific country is also a good way to find potential work in your non-English language countries.

Asking other translators for recommendations is another good way to find reliable agency clients. It's important to exercise discretion if you ask for recommendations from other people in your language pair; small agencies may need only two or three translators in each language combination, and you don't want to encroach on a colleague's main clients. So, it's best to either ask for recommendations from people who do not work in your language pair or to ask colleagues in your language pair to refer you to agencies that they know are actively looking for more translators.

4.1.2 Optimizing your application materials

Remember that your application to an agency is your first exercise in following directions for this potential client. Follow the agency's application instructions to the letter so that your first impression is a good one. Maintain your resumé in several different formats (for example PDF, Microsoft Word and plain text) so that you can send whichever format the agency requests. Always try to include some sort of cover letter; even on an online application form there is often a field for comments or additional information where you can paste a short cover letter.

Bear in mind that you have only a few seconds to grab the attention of the person who is reviewing your application materials. Most small and medium-sized agencies do not have human resources departments, so your resumé is likely to be reviewed by a project manager who is squeezing this task into his or her regular responsibilities. Make it easy for an agency employee to immediately see if you fit what the agency is looking for: put your language pair under your name at the top of the resumé and create an easy-to-read bulleted list of your relevant experience. If you are responding to a specific job announcement, state this in the first sentence of your cover letter; the same is true if you are being referred by a translator who already works for the agency.

4.1.3 Keeping track of your contacts

Once you've sent in your application materials to a potential agency client, make sure to keep a record of the agency's name, the date you applied and any other relevant information. For example, some agencies require that you provide your rates when you apply to them. If you do this, make sure to keep a record of what rates you listed so that you will know how much to charge the agency if they contact you with a project. You can keep your records on paper, in a spreadsheet, or by using a more elaborate contact management software package–the important thing is to log your contacts in a reliable way.

Keep track of the responses that you receive from all of your prospective clients, especially if you receive anything more than an automated "we'll keep your resumé on file" message. If a real person responds to you, even to tell you that the agency has no work for you right now, note this in your contacts file because it is worth following up on. If an agency requests that you follow up with them in a certain amount of time, make sure to note this so that you can do so.

4.1.4 Following up on your contacts

Following up on cold contacts is very important. How much follow up you do will depend on how much time you have and how much you are interested in the potential client. If you have time, try to get your business cards into as many prospective clients' hands as possible. For example, you might send a short handwritten note ("Thank you for responding to my inquiry about working with xyz agency and please let me know if I can help you with any German>English projects in the future") and a couple of business cards to everyone who responds to your initial application. Then you might continue to contact those people every few months afterward.

Mass e-mails are *never* a good way to follow up on your contacts. Even if you want to follow up by e-mail, make sure that the e-mail is addressed to a specific person, and make sure that you have a specific reason for contacting the person. For example, if you receive a positive response to your initial contact but you haven't heard from the agency in a few months, you might contact them to let them know about the major projects you've worked on in case they have anything similar coming in; for example "Over the past few months, I've translated several annual reports for mid-sized companies in the manufacturing sector. I would be happy to work with you on similar projects in the future."

4.2 Marketing to direct clients

Marketing to translation companies is largely a numbers game; if you're qualified and you resolve to apply to five translation companies a day, at some point you'll hit critical mass and work will start coming in. Marketing to direct clients is much more nuanced; there are fewer obvious sources of contacts, you may need to convince clients that hiring you will improve their bottom line and you will need to decide how best to approach these potential clients.

With agency clients, your time will mainly be spent actually applying to potential clients; filling out their online forms and sending out follow-up e-mails. With direct clients, you'll spend much more time researching your potential clients and deciding how best to approach them; a superficial mass-marketing campaign targeting direct clients is unlikely to generate much business for you. So, put a good chunk of time into planning your campaign before you make the initial contact.

One of the keys to direct client marketing is to expand your contacts beyond the translation industry; if you stick with associations, e-mail lists, networking sites etc. that are primarily frequented by other translators, you'll have a hard time finding direct clients. Think about where your prospective direct clients are likely to be getting their business-related information. What associations do they belong to? What trade journals do they read? What online groups do they belong to? Then, position yourself as an information source in those places.

4.2.1 Identifying your target clients

If you want to work with direct clients, you first need to decide what types of clients you'd like to find. In order to do this, you need to be clear on what your specializations are and what types of translation work you like and are good at. If you already work with translation agencies, think of the types of end clients whose documents you work on, and of the types of work you feel most comfortable with. Especially if you are marketing to direct clients for the first time, it's a good idea to stick with the kinds of documents that you have successfully translated many times before; don't take a chance on botching your first direct client interactions.

When you think about your target clients, think about your own work style as well. Do you thrive under pressure or do you avoid rush work at all costs? Do you encourage your clients to call you whenever they need you, or do you like to stick to a 9-5 schedule with weekends off? Do you prefer working with clients in the country where you live, or with international clients? Think about how you can take your own constraints and market them as advantages. For example, if you live in a time zone that is far removed from your clients' time zone, you can offer for them to send you work at the end of the business day so that you translate while they are sleeping and return the work for the start of the next business day. If you are starting a translation business while working another job, you can offer to do night and weekend work whenever your clients need it.

4.2.2 Using your existing network

Undoubtedly the best way to approach a direct client is through a personal referral, either by someone who already freelances for this client or by someone who works in-house for them. So, a good first step in a direct client marketing campaign is to think of people you already know who would be good sources of introductions to potential clients. Obviously, the best kind of personal referral is one where your contact can directly pass your resumé to someone who is in a position to hire you; for example if you have a colleague who works in a different language pair for a direct client that needs translators in your language pair, or if you know someone who works in the international affairs or international marketing department of a large company. However, don't discount people in your network who can either introduce you to pivotal contacts (for example the director of an international chamber of commerce) or who can tell you the name and title of the person at their company who hires translators. Having a specific person to contact is infinitely better than starting your proposal with "Dear Vice President of International Marketing," so make whatever use you can of the contacts you already have.

Offering to work as a backup for translator colleagues who do direct client work is another good way to use your existing network. In this case, you would offer to either subcontract work from your colleague or to have the client work directly with you when your colleague is busy or on vacation.

4.2.3 Expanding your network

If you don't currently have any contacts who can help you find direct clients, or if you've already made use of all of your current contacts, think about expanding your network. In today's work environment, online networking websites such as LinkedIn http://www.linkedin.com offer excellent opportunities for doing this. For example, if you are a member of some LinkedIn groups related to your specializations, you have an excellent source of potential contacts. Look over the profiles of the people who are members of the same LinkedIn groups that you belong to, then send connection requests to the people who look like potential sources of work for you. You don't have to hide your intentions or do a hard sell; you can simply say something like, "I am interested in expanding my network of contacts in the xyz sector/country/etc. and wondered if I might add you to my network."

If you want to pursue this strategy, make sure to do it in a professional and tactful way. *Never* send mass e-mails to multiple potential contacts. Always explain where you found the person's contact information and why you are contacting them.

4.2.4 International business organizations

When you start to research trade associations that your prospective direct clients might belong to, make sure to research international business organizations. International chambers of commerce and world trade associations are excellent places to start, because you can meet prospective clients at the association's networking events and educational sessions and get to know them in a low-pressure situation. In addition, some world trade associations authorize their members to use the association's membership directory for marketing purposes. If you join your local world trade association, you might even offer to present an educational session on best practices for buying translations, or on how businesses can make the most of their translation budgets.

If there is an international (i.e. French-American, German-American etc.) chamber of commerce for your non-English language or non-U.S. country, it may be an excellent source of potential direct clients as well. The appeal of an international chamber of commerce as opposed to a world trade association (assuming you are a freelancer and not an agency or multiple-language vendor) is that you have a higher chance of meeting clients who are in particular need of your language. If you translate from English to Chinese, you may make some excellent contacts at a world trade association, but you will probably also meet lots of companies looking for translators who work in other languages. If you can find a Chinese-American chamber of commerce, you're virtually guaranteed that all of its members have some type of need for Chinese language services.

If there is a world trade association or appropriate international chamber of commerce in your local area, your first step after joining it should be to introduce yourself to the association's president or director. Don't make this a sales pitch; just call or e-mail to introduce yourself as a new member. If you are feeling outgoing or if you get a positive response from the director, invite her or him out to coffee or lunch (at your expense, of course!) in order to learn more about what the association does and how you can fit in.

4.2.5 Your local business news

If you're in the direct client market, it's very important to read and follow your local business news. Nearly every major metropolitan area in the U.S. has at least one local business journal, and many larger cities have several publications worth looking at. You may be able to subscribe to your local business journal for free, and you should at least be able to read the publication's website or receive e-mail updates for free. After you do this for a while, you can decide if it's worth paying for a subscription or not.

If you read your local business news regularly, you will start noticing which companies do business in your non-English language countries. When you see a business news item that alerts you to a potential client ("German solar power company selects Dallas for its flagship U.S. office"), you should look for as many points of contact as possible. Obvious candidates include anyone involved in marketing, international affairs or localization, but make sure to notice whether the article also identifies the local government employee who helped facilitate the deal or the name of a U.S.-based company that the international company will be partnering with. Once you've found some names, start contacting them by e-mail, mail or phone, congratulating the company on its international expansion and offering your services as a high-quality translator or interpreter.

4.2.6 Trade publications

Your local business news will tell you what's happening in the business scene in your area, but you also need to know what is going on beyond your local area, especially in your areas of specialization. Even the advertising sections of these publications are worth reading, since you might find a company advertising services that mesh with what you do. For example, if you see an advertisement for an international freight service that does business in one of your non-English-language countries, it's worth sending your marketing materials to them.

4.2.7 Trade shows

Personal contact with potential clients is very important, and trade shows are an excellent opportunity to meet many potential clients in one place. Trade shows have some downsides; they are often expensive to attend and the popular booths may be very crowded. Also, your potential clients are probably attending the trade show to market their own products and services, not to buy other people's products and services. However, you can get around these issues by offering to volunteer at the trade show in exchange for free or discounted registration (especially if the information desk has a need for your non-English language), and by making contact with some of the attendees before the show. If you contact some companies that look like potential clients, you can raise your chances of success by offering to take their representatives to coffee or lunch if they are available during the show, rather than fighting your way to the front of their booth to try to talk to them.

4.3 Making yourself findable

Your direct client marketing strategy should include both finding potential clients *and* helping potential clients find you. It's important to be findable for at least two reasons: you probably don't have time to send marketing materials to every direct client that could potentially use your services, and there are probably many potential direct clients that you would never think to market to. So, you need to make it as easy as possible for these types of clients to find you. Following are a few tips to help you with this:

- Make sure that you have an active and updated profile on the website of any translators' associations you belong to. List your specializations and write a strong and concise description of what you do and what types of clients you work with. Make sure to keep your contact information updated and revise your profile at least once a year to reflect your current situation.

- Post at least a basic profile on a few online networking websites. In order for potential clients to find you, it's a good idea to have a profile on LinkedIn, a comparable site for your non-English language(s) and any similar sites related to your specializations. These types of sites rank very highly in Internet searches, so it is a real boost to your findability to have a profile on them.

- Use a descriptive e-mail signature. Nearly every e-mail program or web-based e-mail service allows you to include a standard block of text at the bottom of your e-mails. It's a good idea to include at least your language pair(s), website and phone number in your e-mail signature so that everyone who receives an e-mail from you knows what you do. Try to keep your e-mail signature to about four lines so that it does not look like an advertisement. Some translators also use vCard, an electronic version of your business card that can be attached to every e-mail you send.

- Have a website and/or blog and update them regularly. Blogs are an attractive option because they are very quickly indexed by Internet search engines. You can also incorporate a blog into a traditional website so that part of the site is fairly static and part is updated regularly. Make sure to prominently state your language pairs and contact information on your website or blog.

- Write guest posts for other people's blogs. If you don't want to commit to maintaining your own blog or if you want to expand beyond the readership that you have on your own blog, writing for someone else's blog is an excellent option. Make sure that your guest post includes a link back to your own website if you have one; if you don't have a website, you could include a link to your LinkedIn page.

- Write articles for trade publications. Whether you'd like to write for translation industry publications or for publications related to your languages or specializations, articles are a great way to get your name out to potential clients. You can also include articles that you've written in a marketing package to send to potential clients.

- Do pro bono work. This could take the form of volunteering your translation services to worthy organizations (possibly in exchange for some publicity) or volunteering with your local or national translators association. Just make sure that when you take on unpaid work, you treat it as seriously as you would a paid assignment so that you establish a reputation for reliability.

- Do outreach work. Especially if you are involved with your local translators association, there are probably many opportunities to speak at high school and college career fairs, chamber of commerce events and similar gatherings. These are excellent low-pressure opportunities to get to know people outside the translation industry and hand out your business cards.

4.4 Marketing materials

A freelance translator's most basic marketing materials are a well-written resumé and cover letter, but there is definitely a place for other marketing materials as well, especially if you are marketing to direct clients. Given the widespread availability of high-quality and low-cost marketing pieces, it's worth experimenting to see what materials might be useful to you.

Marketing collateral pieces are very helpful when you attend a conference or trade show, because most of the other attendees probably have fairly generic marketing materials. At a translators association conference, virtually all of the attendees will bring a resumé on white or off-white paper and some traditional business cards, so even something simple like a marketing postcard can help you stand out.

Postcards are a low-cost piece of marketing collateral. Expect to pay 10-25 cents per postcard for four-color double sided postcards from online printers such as VistaPrint, Overnight Prints, or Got Print. If you take the time to make them attractive, your potential clients may keep them for that reason alone. Postcards are easy to store and to hand over to people, and you don't need a huge amount of text and graphics to make a nice looking postcard. You can also use postcards to follow up with people after conferences and trade shows by writing a personal message on the back.

Brochures are another reasonable marketing option, but they are more expensive to create, require more text and graphics and are physically less durable than postcards. If you enjoy graphic design, don't mind hiring a graphic designer or know someone who could help you with the design, brochures can be a good option because they allow you to include much more information than you can put on a postcard.

Once you progress beyond postcards and brochures, there are a dizzying array of marketing collateral possibilities ranging from small and inexpensive (ballpoint pens, magnets) to larger and more expensive (personalized flash drives, desk calendars). On the one hand, these items can be useful because you have something durable to give to prospective clients, and everyone can use these types of items. On the other hand, a cheap pen or notepad is unlikely to make much of an impression on a high-paying client. For these types of clients, you may be better off selecting a less generic type of gift.

4.5 Creating a website

Whether you are looking for clients in your local area or worldwide, a website is an excellent way to market your freelance services. In the past, it was difficult and expensive to create a professional-looking website and few translators had a good website. Now, if you're reasonably tech-savvy you can create a basic but professional business website yourself.

A simple website can serve as a virtual brochure for your services, and a more complicated website can include a blog, contact or project quote forms, sample translations and more. If you don't currently have a website, it's probably best to start with a brochure-style site that features your services, experience and contact information. If you already have a website, you might want to think about adding some more interactive features such as a blog.

Remember to follow a few basic rules of good web design:

- Don't have pages that scroll to infinity; you should set your web pages up so that they require little or no scrolling to view the whole page.

- Don't use huge image files or animations; go with smaller, faster-loading graphics and make sure to include ALT tags (text tags that appear if someone has the images turned off in their browser or is using a browser for the visually impaired). Make sure that your site's code validates, meaning that it is compliant with current standards for web page code.

- Don't bury the important information; visitors to your website should be able to find your name, language pair(s) and contact information without clicking through layers of links to get to it.

- Make sure that your site is readable; check the font, font size and colors in a variety of web browsers. If you want to use a background on your pages, make sure that it doesn't obscure the text on the page.

- Conduct some basic usability testing on your own site. Ask a few friends to browse your site and tell you if they can easily and quickly find the information that a prospective client would be looking for.

- Make sure that all of the pages on your site have a consistent theme; use the same color scheme, font and basic design for all of your pages.

- If you have time-sensitive information on your website (for example "News," "Availability," "Recent projects," etc.) make sure to keep it updated so that your site does not look stale.

When it comes to actually creating your site, you have a variety of options. You can pay a professional web designer to create the site for you, you can create it yourself and hand-code the HTML, or you can create it yourself using a content management tool such as WordPress http://www.wordpress.com or a site building tool that comes with your hosting package. The best way to find a good website designer is to ask for referrals from people who have websites that you like. If you decide to hire a web designer, be prepared to spend real money if you want a site that is unique-looking and really captures the feel of your business. You should expect to spend at least $1,000 if you want some custom design elements and a non-generic looking site. If you have less than $500 to spend, you are probably best off either paying a web designer to teach you how to build the site yourself, or spending the money on custom artwork that will make your site stand out.

4.6 Resources

- Get Clients Now (marketing book and courses for free-lancers): http://www.getclientsnow.com

- The Entrepreneurial Linguist (book by Judy and Dagmar Jenner): http://www.entrepreneuriallinguist.com

- Fidus Interpres (book by Fabio Said, in Portuguese): http://www.fidusinterpres.com

- The Prosperous Translator (book by Chris Durban): http://www.prosperoustranslator.com

- WordPress (blog and website-building software and plat-forms): http://www.wordpress.com and http://www.wordpress.org

- Guerrilla Marketing: `http://www.gmarketing.com`

- Seth Godin's Blog (marketing tips):
  `http://www.sethgodin.typepad.com`

- Creative Freelancer Blog:
  `http://www.creativefreelancerblog.com`

5 Online networking and social media

Increasing your name recognition and building a network of colleagues you trust are key to your success as a freelancer. Fortunately, the Internet offers some excellent options; whether you hate the thought of attending a Chamber of Commerce in-person networking event or you're simply looking for ways to reach out further than you can in person, online networking and social media are worth some of your marketing time.

Online networking can take many forms; if you're a member of a local or national translators association, you are likely to be able to participate in its online discussion forum or e-mail list. Translation marketplaces like ProZ http://www.proz.com and TranslatorsCafé http://www.translatorscafe.com have a wide variety of forums that you can participate in and get to know other translators, and general professional networking portals such as LinkedIn http://www.linkedin.com, Xing http://www.xing.com and Viadeo http://www.viadeo.com can allow you to meet not only other translators but people who work in your areas of specialization. Social media has become its own category in the online networking universe; blogs, podcasts and social networking sites such as Facebook http://www.facebook.com and Twitter http://www.twitter.com can be either a major time waster or an excellent source of contacts and information, depending on how you use them. Let's take a look at the current popular online networking and social media opportunities and how freelance translators can best make use of them.

5.1 Listserves and e-mail discussion lists

Listserves and e-mail discussion lists are normally restricted to people who belong to a certain group or association; they are often managed using services such as Yahoo Groups or Google Groups. For example, most local translators' associations and most divisions of the American Translators Association have their own listserves which members can join for free. For most listserves, you can choose the frequency with which you receive new messages from the list; you can usually choose to receive every message when it comes out, or to receive a daily digest of messages, or not to receive any messages by e-mail, in which case you can visit the listserve's web page to read the messages whenever you choose.

Whatever your language pair, specialization, technology platform or niche market, there's a good chance that you can find a listserve of like-minded people to join. The fact that most listserves are for members only is both an asset and a liability. It's nice to be able to send your message to a restricted group of people, for example people who work in your language combination or who are freelancers working in your local area. But unfortunately, messages that you send to a listserve may have a limited lifespan of availability and limited distribution; a listserve is a great place to ask specific questions or offer specific pieces of information, but it is less helpful for posting information that you would like to distribute or make searchable to a wide audience. Depending on the service used to host the listserve, it may be difficult or even impossible for people to consult the list archives, which can result in the same questions being asked many times. However, for translators who live in remote areas or in countries where their source or target languages are not widely spoken, listserves are a great way to strike up relationships with other translators because you can get to know people fairly directly. At the very least, you should plan to join the listserves associated with the translators associations that you belong to.

5.2 Online forums

Online forums are similar to listserves in that they are mostly used for posting and answering questions, but online forums are usually public and hosted on a website. For example, the large translation portals such as ProZ and TranslatorsCafé have a huge range of forums that anyone can read for free. These are great resources for finding information because the archives stay on line indefinitely. Many forums are not moderated or restricted, meaning that anyone can post to them. While this gives you access to a wider audience of readers and contributors, bear in mind that the quality of information posted to a forum is only as good as the person who posted it; and anything you post to a forum can, in theory, be read by anyone on the Internet—so don't use a public forum to complain about your clients if you want to keep them!

5.3 Social networking sites

Social networking sites come in a variety of flavors and are a helpful addition to the freelance translator's networking arsenal, but it's important to know how to use these sites correctly and not to let them become endless time drains. Let's look at a few of the more popular social networking sites and their uses:

5.3.1 LinkedIn

The most popular professionally-oriented social networking site is LinkedIn http://www.linkedin.com. Its members cover almost every conceivable industry and specialization. LinkedIn functions using the classic "profile and connections" social networking model. After joining LinkedIn, you build a profile with your current and past work information, education and other vital details and then invite people to join your network. You can also post a status update to let your network know what you're working on, and you can change the status update as often as you want.

As of 2011, LinkedIn offers four types of accounts: Personal (free), Business ($24.95 per month or $249.50 per year), Business-Plus ($49.95 per month or $499.50 per year) and Pro ($499.95 per month or $4,999.50 per year). The major difference between these accounts is how and how often you can add people to your LinkedIn network. For example, LinkedIn has a proprietary feature called InMail that allows you to send an e-mail to someone outside your LinkedIn network; however, this feature is only available if you have a paid LinkedIn account. With a free Personal account you can receive unlimited InMails, but you can only send InMails if you have a paid account.

For most freelancers, LinkedIn's free Personal account is probably adequate; unless you want to use LinkedIn to market to a lot of people you don't already know, you can build a good profile and network with the free account. LinkedIn is useful for a few purposes: to create a "virtual Rolodex" of your contacts (this is especially helpful so that you don't have to keep track of e-mail addresses for people who you contact infrequently) and to make it easier for prospective clients to find you. Here are a few tips for building a strong LinkedIn profile:

- Use the same name that you use professionally. It's important to choose one and only one name that you will use professionally. Make sure that you use this name for your LinkedIn profile.

- Add a professional-looking photograph. LinkedIn gives you the option to upload a photo and it's a good idea to do so, because it personalizes your profile and makes you more recognizable, especially if you have a common name.

- Write a descriptive tag line. Your tag line will appear every time you appear in a LinkedIn search result or as a suggested connection for someone else, so make sure that it gives a good description of what you do. Unfortunately, LinkedIn's profile builder is not very freelancer-friendly because it requires you to enter something in the "Company" field. If you don't enter a company name, you may appear as "Self-employed at Full-time freelance translator," which looks a little clunky in search results.

- State your most important information first. You'll be asked to enter a succinct description of what services you provide. Don't count on a prospective client reading your entire profile to find out if you're a good fit for them. It's advisable to put your language pair(s), specialization(s) and geographic location (if relevant to your work) in your first sentence; for example, "Dallas-based Spanish to English translator and conference interpreter specializing in the medical and pharmaceutical industries," or "English to French translator specializing in legal and financial translations, working with clients throughout the U.S. and Europe."

- Create a custom URL for your profile by clicking the "Edit" link on the "Public Profile" line of your profile.

- If you have a blog, feed it to your LinkedIn profile. On your Profile, scroll down to the Applications section and click "Add Application," then find the application for your blog hosting service. Doing this not only gives your blog more exposure, but it adds fresh content to your profile with no additional effort on your part.

- Ask for recommendations. LinkedIn allows you to solicit recommendations from your connections. Although you can send a mass e-mail to all of your connections, it's advisable to ask specific people to recommend you, possibly suggesting a specific aspect of your work for them to comment on.

- Either update your status regularly or don't update it at all. LinkedIn's status update feature can be an effective way of sharing information with your network, but your profile will have a stale look if you only update your status every few months. Update your status at least once a week if possible.

Once you've built a decent basic profile on LinkedIn, you should start adding connections. There are a few ways to find people you'd like to connect with; you can allow LinkedIn to search your e-mail address book, you can add connections manually by typing people's names into the Search box, or you can add connections through LinkedIn Groups (more on Groups below). Once you click "Add (name of person) to your network," a dialog box will pop up with the text of a message to be sent to the person you'd like to connect with. Personalize this message by either including a greeting if you know the person well, such as "I've just joined LinkedIn, looking forward to connecting with you here!" or reminding the person how you know them: "We met at last year's ATA conference, may I add you as a connection?" People have different theories about who you should connect with on LinkedIn; some people connect only with people who they know well in "real life," some connect with people who they meet at conferences and work-related events, while others consider themselves "open networkers" and will connect with almost anyone. Unless you want to connect with anyone who asks, it's helpful to formulate a connection strategy in advance: do you want to connect only with people who you actually know, or also with people who you may run into only once? Do you want to focus your connection efforts on colleagues and existing clients, or on prospective clients? Thinking about these issues up front will help you get the most out of your efforts on LinkedIn.

LinkedIn Groups are definitely worth exploring. Groups are very similar to online forums, but most LinkedIn Groups require you to be approved as a member in order to read the group archives or post something to the group. You can search for Groups you want to join by using the site's search feature; also take a look at the profiles of people you work with and see which Groups they belong to (Groups are normally displayed in someone's profile). There are a lot of translation-related LinkedIn Groups, but you can probably get the most return for your efforts by joining Groups related to your specializations. For example, if you join a Group for patent attorneys, you may be the only translator in the Group, so you're automatically the translation industry expert. Also, you can easily start a discussion within your Group and ask a question about translation; for example "What are some pitfalls and best practices of working with a translator in this industry?" This will help you get to know the other people in the Group and find out how your services might be helpful to them.

For each LinkedIn Group you join, make sure to abide by that Group's policies on marketing announcements and job postings. Most Groups have an area where these types of postings are allowed, but make sure to restrict your marketing efforts to that designated area so that you don't annoy Group members and/or get banned from the Group. Once you've joined LinkedIn, you'll receive (unless you de-select this option in your settings) a periodic "news feed" about what is going on in your network. For example, this news feed tells you who joined a new Group, who added new connections, who posted a status update, etc. In order to keep your name fresh in your connections' minds, try to do something that causes you to appear in this news feed every week; updating your status regularly is an easy way to do this. You can also get some metrics about your LinkedIn visibility by looking at the "Who's viewed my profile?" box on your LinkedIn home page which will tell you how many people have looked at your profile recently and how many times you have appeared in search results on LinkedIn.

5.3.2 Facebook

Facebook http://www.facebook.com is a hugely popular social networking site; for freelance translators and interpreters, Facebook is probably more applicable to your personal life than to your professional life, but it's still worth a look. Facebook uses the same general model as LinkedIn; you have a personal profile and then you add contacts (Friends). In addition, you can create Facebook pages that are separate from your profile. Then, people can become "Fans" of your Facebook page much as they would become Friends on your personal page. The upside of Facebook is that it has an enormous user base; it's a great way to spread the word about what you're doing, reconnect with people you know, and share information, photos, video etc. Facebook has a few negatives as well; the site's privacy policy seems to change frequently and without warning (for example, as related to how Facebook can use the content that you post to your page). Also, many people on Facebook really blur the line between what is personal and what is appropriate for business, and unless you spend a significant amount of time customizing your settings, you have very little control over what other people post to your Wall (the public area of your profile). With Facebook, it's especially important to have a plan before you start. If you decide that you are going to restrict your Facebook Friend base to only people who you are personal friends with, have a strategy for what you will do when a business contact wants to add you as a Friend. For example, you might respond "I find LinkedIn more useful for my work contacts" and then you might add that person as a LinkedIn connection instead.

5.3.3 Twitter

Twitter http://www.twitter.com is technically known as a micro-blogging service. On Twitter, you post "Tweets," status updates of 140 characters or less which are sent out to people in your network, who are referred to as "Followers." One useful aspect of Twitter is that you can have one-way relationships; just because someone is following you doesn't mean that you are obligated to follow them. Twitter also allows you to use hash tags (#) to tag key words in your Tweets, for example "Finishing a rush #translation for tomorrow;" these hash tags are then searchable on the website http://www.hashtags.org. Twitter also offers the option of feeding your Tweets into other social media outlets that you use; for example you can feed your Tweets to Facebook and LinkedIn so that they appear as your Facebook or LinkedIn status; most blog hosting services also offer you the option of having your Tweets appear in the sidebar of your blog. There's no question that there's a lot of "noise" on Twitter; however, the fact that it's very easy to post Tweets and the fact that many people use their mobile phones to receive Tweets makes Twitter a great way to get information out very quickly.

5.3.4 Blogs

Blogs are a type of website, and the distinction between blogs and static websites is not always clear. Blogs are generally more interactive and updated more often than standard websites are. For example, most bloggers post new content to their blog frequently, anywhere from once a week to several times a day, and most bloggers also allow and even encourage their readers to post comments on the articles that appear on the blog. Whether you read and comment on other people's blogs or write your own blog, the "blogosphere" (online blog world) is definitely worth exploring.

Until recently, most websites were informational one-way streets; the author publishing the information didn't have the means (or often the desire) to spark a discussion among equals. The major change brought about by blogging is that a blog post can be the start of open-ended discussion; once the blogger publishes a post, readers can add comments that continue or critique the discussion in the post. In addition, because blogs are easy to update, they are often sources of breaking news or of commentary on breaking news. Blogs are an excellent networking tool for freelance translators because they offer you a way to join discussions among colleagues from all over the world. Translators have proven to be very enthusiastic bloggers (unfortunately the same is not yet true of interpreters!), as have many other language workers such as journalists, editors and marketing consultants.

If you visit a blog and find a post that interests you or about which you have something to say, click the link that allows you to add a comment to that post (there may or may not already be comments on the post). Most blog hosting services require you to supply your e-mail address when you post a comment, but it is not normally displayed along with the comment; if you have a website, you can choose to enter its address when you post a comment, and your name will then be hyperlinked to your website when people view your comment.

The complexity of posting a comment depends partially on the blog's hosting service and partially on the settings that the individual blogger has chosen; you may be able to post a comment simply by entering your name and e-mail address and clicking "Submit," or you may have to create some sort of account or even wait for the blogger to moderate (approve) your comment. Commenting on other people's blogs is a great way to dip your toe in the blogosphere. By commenting, you can offer useful information to other people who read the blog without taking on the commitment of writing your own blog. You'll find that a lot of blog posts involve lists of tips: how to write an effective marketing e-mail, best places to find new clients, top five laptop computers for translators, and so on. If you have a tip to add to one of these lists, submit it as a comment; your tip will then be available for other blog readers to look at, and if you have a website, people may find it because of the tip that you posted. The blogosphere is a lot like an online roundtable. In much the same way as your local translators association might have an in-person session where various translators offer advice about marketing, networking, technology or translation techniques, you'll find people discussing all of these topics on their blogs. It's interesting to compare perspectives from translators in different countries and cultures, and it's also interesting to see what people think of the opinions that you post.

The importance of using a feed reader

If you find a few blogs that you would like to read regularly, a feed reader can really help you keep track of updates to these blogs and control how much time you spend reading them. Some of the more popular feed readers are Google Reader http://www.google.com/reader and the Sage plugin for the Firefox web browser. Once you choose a feed reader, you enter a blog's URL to subscribe to its feed, which means the new items that are posted to it. Then, instead of having to visit 12 or 25 different websites a day to see if your favorite blogs have been updated, you can just scan over your feed reader, which will display the headlines of the new posts on the blogs that you're subscribed to. It's your choice if you want to click on the headlines to read the whole post, or if you just want to scan the brief preview that the feed reader displays. A feed reader is very useful because you can comment on blog posts as soon as they appear (rather than waiting until the post has already been online for some time) and you can follow a lot of blogs but spend minimal time keeping up with them.

5.4 Using social media effectively

Depending on how you use it, social media can be either a highly effective addition to your marketing and networking strategy or a colossal waste of time. It's important to have a social media strategy so that you know what your social media goals are before you jump in.

I had written a fairly successful e-newsletter about translation technology (Open Source Update) for several years before blogs came on the scene. I really enjoyed writing the newsletter because it was a great way to combine my interests in translation, writing and technology. Over the years, the newsletter's mailing list had grown to around 500 subscribers, so I knew that people were interested in reading the content, but it required a fair bit of work to keep the mailing list up to date (for example managing new subscriptions and removals). So, writing my own blog seemed like a good way to pursue this idea while eliminating a lot of the administrative work.

I've found that my blog is perhaps the best marketing and networking tool that I've ever implemented; it has allowed me to develop relationships with translators around the world and has attracted readers who are interested in the other aspects of my business such as this book and the online course that I teach. At the same time, I've found that I have to really limit the amount of time I spend on social media every day, because there's the potential for it to encroach on my other business activities. I have a feed reader set up and I spend only 10-15 minutes reading new blog posts each morning, much the same way that some people scan the headlines of a printed newspaper. I spend a similar amount of time on LinkedIn, updating my status, adding new contacts and reading Group discussions, partially because I find that these are good ways to find new direct clients. I use Facebook only for personal contacts and I post to Twitter no more than once a day, not because I don't think it could be useful but because at some point I also have to do my real job which is translation.

Unless you intend to earn money from your social media efforts (which isn't out of the question, for example by selling advertising on your blog), it's critical to decide a few things before you begin. By entering the social media world, are you hoping to find new clients, and if so who are they? Are you hoping to build relationships with other translators who you can share work with, or would you just like an efficient way of sharing and gathering information on-line? All of these considerations will help you decide which social media platforms are right for you and how much time you should invest in them.

5.5 Resources

- LinkedIn: `http://www.linkedin.com`

- LinkedIn's blog (tips for using the site):
  `http://www.blog.linkedin.com`

- Twitter: `http://www.twitter.com`

- Twitter for Business: `http://www.business.twitter.com`

- Facebook: `http://www.facebook.com`

- Google Reader: `http://google.com/reader`

- Viadeo (similar to LinkedIn, oriented toward the European market): `http://www.viadeo.com`

- Ning (allows you to set up your own social networks):
  `http://www.ning.com`

- Mashable (social media news): http://www.mashable.com

- Blogging with Beth (social media consulting for freelancers and entrepreneurs): http://www.bloggingwithbeth.com

- Lexiophiles Top 100 Language Blogs:
  http://www.lexiophiles.com

- Suggested translation-related blogs:

    - About Translation:
      http://www.aboutranslation.blogspot.com

    - Fidus Interpres (in English, Portuguese and German):
      http://www.fidusinterpres.com

    - Mox's Blog (cartoons about translation!):
      http://mox.ingenierotraductor.com

    - Musings from an Overworked Translator:
      http://www.translationmusings.com

    - Naked Translations (in English and French):
      http://www.nakedtranslations.com/en/blog

    - Not Just Another Translator:
      http://anothertranslator.eu

    - There's Something about Translation:
      http://www.dillonslattery.com

    - Thoughts on Translation:
      http://www.thoughtsontranslation.com

    - Transblawg: http://www.transblawg.eu

    - Translate This!: http://blog.wahlster.net

    - Translation Times:
      http://www.translationtimes.com

    - Translation Tribulations:
      http://www.translationtribulations.com

6 Home office setup, technology and translation memory software

6.1 Preparing your home office

While it's possible to spend many thousands of dollars setting up an office for your freelance translation business, it's equally possible to get going with a minimal investment while maintaining a professional image. Most translators work from home, so there's no stigma attached to doing so. At the same time, working from home poses its own set of challenges, including but not limited to: knowing how to manage your time so that your business is profitable; knowing when to take breaks and how to get enough exercise; resisting the temptation to work either too little or too much; setting boundaries for kids or other people in your household; staying on task and setting priorities.

6.2 The ups and downs of working from home

If your current job involves a long commute, inconvenient hours or an unpleasant work environment, the thought of being largely on your own schedule and wearing whatever you want to work can seem like a slice of paradise. For many translators who work from home, the situation is an all-around win. They have more control over their schedules, can work at times of the day when they have the most energy and can devote more time to their families and non-work interests. At the same time, other freelance translators fail at self-employment primarily because they cannot work productively from home.

If working from home is really not for you, consider looking for an in-house job. In the U.S., government agencies such as the FBI, CIA and NSA are probably your best option if you are a beginner. However, in most cases you'll find the most work opportunities and highest pay by working for yourself. Many work-from-home consultants identify a few key personality traits that successful independent professionals share, for example: they are self-starters or "go-getters" who need very little external motivation; they understand their own positives and negatives; they are able to make good decisions quickly; they are energized by healthy competition rather than feeling intimidated by it, and they have a high level of self-discipline and will-power.

You'll want to assess where you stand on the issues presented by these questions, and also consider how well your current life situation lends itself to working independently from a home office. For example, do you have a location in your home that can be used as a home office? Keep in mind that in most cases, in order to tax-deduct your home office expenses, your office must be a separate area that is used exclusively as an office. So if you set up your computer in a corner of the guest room, for tax purposes it's not an office. Does your family or living situation lend itself to working productively from home? Can you set guidelines for your spouse, roommate or children on times that you are "at work" and not available except in the case of an emergency? If you have small children, can you afford to pay for child care while you work, even if you're not making a lot of money at the start? If you're planning on translation as your primary source of income, do you have six to nine months' income in savings to live off while the business gets going? It's important to consider these issues before you find yourself in a bad situation, and to see the relationship between planning and business success.

6.3 Necessary office equipment

Even if you need to purchase some pieces of computer or office equipment, startup expenses for a freelance translation business should be relatively modest. If you already have an appropriate computer and a place to work from, your expenses might add up to only a few hundred dollars. Whether you have them already or not, here are a few items that make up the basic translation home office.

A computer is absolutely essential to a translator's work, and for backup purposes you may even want or need more than one computer. If you're prone to repetitive strain injury from typing, you may want to consider an ergonomic keyboard, although opinions differ on whether these work for everyone. If you live in an area where wireless Internet access is available in public places, a laptop with Wi-Fi capabilities can be a great way to escape the home office when you feel isolated.

A reliable backup system. Whether you use an external hard drive, removable media such as DVDs or an online service such as Carbonite, you absolutely must back up your computer system or risk losing your business. One simple option is to use a web-based e-mail account to store files that you need immediate access to in the event of a computer crash. You can e-mail yourself the most recent version of all of your in-progress projects at the end of every day, and then use one of the options listed above to do a full backup of your system less often, maybe every two to three days.

A large computer monitor is also important, in order to minimize the amount of time you spend scrolling up and down. Many translators use two or even three monitors; one for the source document and one for the target, or one for the translation memory program and one for an online reference. Your computer may require an additional video card to accomodate a second monitor, but most newer computers will support two monitors directly.

A comfortable desk and chair. You're going to be spending 90% or more of your time sitting at your desk, so make it comfortable and correctly sized for you; using your kitchen table or a card table isn't a great idea. Without a desk and chair that fit you, it can be tiring and uncomfortable to sit in the same position for hours at a time.

A phone. Whether or not you want or need a dedicated business phone line, it's crucial to be able to identify which calls are for your business so that you can answer the phone professionally. One option offered by most phone service providers is a *custom ring* number (sometimes called a *distinctive ring* number), which is an additional phone number that runs over the same physical line as your existing phone number. When a call comes to your business phone number, the phone will ring differently (normally two short rings instead of one long one), so that you know that the call is work related. A hands-free telephone headset can be really helpful when you need to type and talk at the same time, and you can purchase one inexpensively at an office supply store.

A place to keep files. You'll need a filing box or cabinet to keep invoices, check stubs, tax information, hard copy translation documents, client information etc.

Internet access is another essential element of the translation home office. Broadband Internet via cable, DSL or satellite is a necessity.

A bookcase for dictionaries. Ideally, this should be within arm's reach of your desk so that you're not constantly getting up to get a book.

6.4 Organizing your business

When setting up your office, prepare for your business to grow. Following are some tips for organizing your translation business for maximum productivity.

Keep track of your assignments. When you only have one or two clients, it's easy to remember which assignment is due when; add in five or ten others, and it's impossible. In order to avoid missing deadlines, make sure to log every project as it comes in, ideally in more than one place. For example, you might keep a spreadsheet using different color codes for each client, and record the project description, due date and rate of pay. Then you could also keep a calendar next to your desk, with upcoming deadlines written in it. With this double-entry system, you're less likely to forget a deadline.

Keep track of your billings and collections. Without this simple step, you will soon have no business at all. Every time you issue an invoice, record the date, client's name, invoice number, amount of the invoice and date due. Again, you can record this information either electronically, by using a spreadsheet or accounting software, or on paper. When a client pays you, note this wherever you recorded the invoice information, and also file the check stub or invoice marked "paid" in a folder for that client.

Keep track of your business expenses. Depending on your tax and living situation, some or all of your business expenses such as office supplies, Internet access, auto mileage, phone bills, and even home office expenses like a portion of your mortgage payment and utilities may be tax deductible. However, you can get in serious tax trouble for deducting these expenses without having accurate records such as receipts and an auto mileage log.

Choose a reliable accounting system. There are a variety of ways to do your office bookkeeping, from a paper ledger book to a spreadsheet to a full-spectrum accounting software package. Whatever you choose, they key is to use your system consistently so that you don't end up wondering how much money you actually made or how much you spent on office expenses.

Keep only one calendar. One of the beautiful things about working from home is that you're not usually on a set schedule; one of the downsides of this is the tendency to double-book appointments or deadlines so that you end up scheduling a phone conference and a dentist appointment at the same time. Keep one calendar with personal and work appointments and deadlines to avoid conflicts.

Use a prioritized to-do list. One of the keys to remaining productive, especially in a home office setup, is to avoid interrupting your work to perform the many small administrative tasks that come up. When you remember something that you need to do, such as send out an invoice, respond to an e-mail, or update your website, don't perform the task right then unless absolutely necessary. Instead, record it, either on paper or electronically and prioritize it, for example as low/medium/high, or today/this week/when time allows. Then when you need a break from working, tackle the tasks in order of priority.

File! Instead of piling things on your desk to be lost, recycled, etc., force yourself to file anything that you're not using immediately. For example, keep a file for receipts to be entered into your business expense log, then transfer the receipts to a file for that year's business expenses once you've entered them.

6.5 Resources

- Rat Race Rebellion (information on working from home): http://www.ratracerebellion.com

- Two Minute Commute (more tips on working from home): http://2minutecommute.com

- LifeOrganizers (office organization tips): http://www.lifeorganizers.com

- All Business (general tips on running a small business): http://www.allbusiness.com

7 Research tools and methods

Along with target-language writing skills, research is one of a translator's core competencies. No good translator works without using dictionaries, websites, terminology databases, listserves and other reference materials to ensure that the finished translation is as accurate as possible. Some translators prefer paper dictionaries and own a wide variety of specialized terminology resources; others have created a mobile office that makes use of online and CD-based dictionaries and still others prefer to research terms in context in previously published documents. The method you choose is up to you; the important thing about terminology research is to do it!

7.1 Sources for printed dictionaries

Even as information becomes increasingly electronic, print dictionaries are a valuable and indispensable resource. When it comes to specialized terminology in a particular subject area, online resources are often much less comprehensive than their printed counterparts. You should be able to obtain basic bilingual dictionaries at any large bookstore. For more specialized bilingual dictionaries and for monolingual dictionaries (for example a Japanese to Japanese synonym dictionary), you will probably have to use the services of a foreign language or translation-specific bookstore. There are a few such sources in the United States:

- InTrans Book Service http://www.intransbooks.com is currently the best source for translation-specific books in English, Spanish, German and Portuguese. All of its inventory is available by mail order. InTrans has a booth at most conferences sponsored by the American Translators Association, and is a great source for both basic dictionaries and obscure, specialized and hard-to-find volumes.

- Schoenhof's Foreign Books http://www.schoenhofs.com, which has a brick and mortar store in Cambridge, MA and also sells by mail, is a good option for both dictionaries and for monolingual foreign language materials.

- Multilingual Books http://www.multilingualbooks.com is a brick and mortar store in Seattle and also has a comprehensive online site. They are a good resource for language learning materials and foreign films.

7.2 Web-based research tools

Web-based terminology resources have a major place in a translator's arsenal of research tools. Web-based dictionaries and glossaries have the advantage of being easily updatable and easily searchable, but it is important to cast a critical eye on a web-based resource's reliability. Online terminology resources that include user-generated content require that you use your judgment when looking at the terminology suggestions. Some entries may be excellent because they are contributed by experienced translators, while others may be contributed by people with limited knowledge of what they're writing about. Whenever possible, try to verify these types of terms by finding another resource that agrees or disagrees with what you've already found.

There are also various official terminology resources online, such as websites maintained by governments and official language regulation entities. These can be very valuable resources, especially if you can find parallel texts (the same text in more than one language) in your language pairs.

7.3 What to research

One of the hardest things about working as a translator is knowing what you don't know; accuracy requires knowing when to research a term or concept. Following are some items that require research, and some suggestions on how to go about this.

Any word that you don't recognize. If you come upon a word you don't know, don't guess at it! Many terms may appear in your basic dictionary and you'll be done with your research very quickly.

Acronyms and abbreviations. Some acronyms and abbreviations are obvious in certain contexts, such as NASA in an aeronatics industry contract or UN in a diplomatic document. Others will be less obvious, and can be complicated by the fact that some international organizations use one name in all languages and some use a translated version of their names. Company-specific acronyms and abbreviations are another challenge, and will often require contacting the translation's end client for explanation of these terms.

Titles. Many official titles can be translated more than one way, such as the terms "President," "Chairman" and "Chief Executive Officer" for the head of a company. It is important to find out if the company has used standard titles for its employees in the past, and if so what they are. Some companies have bilingual websites that are very helpful in this regard, and sometimes you will have to create your terms from scratch.

Names of organizations. As noted previously, some international organizations go by one name in every language, while others have a standard translation of their name that is used in other languages. It is important to find out if the organization's name is normally translated or not, and if so, what the standard translation is.

People's names. Especially for translators working in languages that do not use the Roman alphabet (for example Arabic, Chinese, Japanese etc.), it is important to follow standard conventions for the transliteration of names from and into English.

Specialization-specific usage. Once you've discovered the correct term, it's important to make sure that you are using it properly. For example, to a computer professional, the expression "data on the server" might be preferable to the expression "data in the server;" or a finance professional might prefer the term "500 euro" to "500 euros" in certain contexts. If you search for those expressions in English, ignoring the translation component, your translation will be more accurate.

7.4 Resources

- InTrans Books: `http://www.intransbooks.com`

- Schoenhof's Foreign Books: `http://www.schoenhofs.com`

8 Translation technology

8.1 The role of technology in translation

If you tell someone at a networking event that you're a translator, there's a good chance that the person will respond, "I thought that computers did all that now!" Although computers aren't likely to put human translators out of business anytime soon, technology plays a crucial and growing role in the work that human translators do. Many translators struggle to master the technology that can help them work more efficiently and more consistently. This probably isn't surprising given that many experienced translators started their careers using typewriters; if you are tech-savvy, you'll have a leg up on many of your freelance competitors!

8.2 Translation home office technology

Aside from translation memory software and possibly speech recognition software, the translation home office does not usually include out-of-the-ordinary technology. If you already work in a career where you use a computer, you probably know most of what it takes to run a translation home office. If your current job does not involve computer use, you may want to invest in a library or community college course in basic computer skills. Regardless of what your translation specializations are, every translator should know:

How to use advanced e-mail features. You should know what a *read receipt* is and how to request one or send one; how to *carbon copy* (CC) and *blind carbon copy* (BCC) someone on an e-mail and when to use both of these features; how to send and receive attachments; how to copy a text document and paste it into the body of an e-mail, and how to use *reply all* and *reply to sender* on e-mails that are sent to more than one person.

Sending and receiving attachments. You will receive and return most translation projects as e-mail attachments, so it's important to know how to attach a file to an e-mail and how to download an attachment when you receive one. It's also important to know where to find an attachment if your spam filter catches the message it's attached to. In addition, you should know how to use a program such as WinZip to zip groups of files into one attachment, and how to unzip these attachments when you receive them. It's also helpful to know how to password-protect your zip files.

How to format documents. Often, clients will want their translated documents to look as much as possible like the source documents, so that the reader has the impression of looking at the same document in another language. To achieve this, it's important to know how to use different fonts, text boxes and tables in a word processor in order to properly format documents. Taking a class in advanced Microsoft Word or OpenOffice features can save you a lot of time when you need to format complex documents.

How to fill out and submit an online form. Especially if you will be applying to agencies, it's important to know how to use drop-down menus and text fields, how to paste your resumé into the appropriate field on an online form, and to remember to hit that Submit button only once! You should also have some basic knowledge of how browser features such as cookies work, without which you won't be able to navigate certain websites.

How to use *Track Changes* in a word processor. In the translation industry, the standard word processor is Microsoft Word, so if you use another word processor such as WordPerfect or OpenOffice.org, make sure that the program can save files in Microsoft Word format. For sending and receiving editing comments on your documents, you should know how to use Microsoft Word's *Track Changes* feature to make corrections and insert comments.

How to effectively search online. Often during a translation assignment, you'll come across a term that isn't in any dictionary you use. The next step is to search for the term online and see what you find. You should know how to evaluate the trustworthiness of a website, how to use bilingual websites, and which search engines work best for you.

How to use web browser bookmarks. For sites you visit all the time, or visit once and want to remember, it's important to have a system of organized bookmarks stored in your web browser.

How to organize folders on your computer. Starting out with a folder called "Translation" isn't a bad idea, but once you have multiple clients with multiple projects, your files will quickly become impossible to find without a system of organized folders for each client and project.

How to rename a file. When you perform a translation, the client will often want you to translate the file name as well.

How to find a file. Once you've been translating for a few years or maybe even a few months, your hard drive will be filled with hundreds or thousands of files. Knowing how to effectively use the advanced features of *Find→File* or the equivalent on your computer is crucial.

How to back up your computer. This certainly isn't the most alluring aspect of home office computing, but it is arguably the most crucial. Since a translator is nearly 100% dependent on having a functional computer in order to work, think about what you would do if your computer simply wouldn't turn on one morning, if the hard drive died, or if the computer itself were destroyed by a flood or fire. A simple backup system might entail e-mailing yourself copies of projects in progress so that you can work on them from another computer. More advanced systems, which are an excellent idea, involve using some sort of removable device like a USB flash drive, Zip drive, CD-RW/DVD-RW, external hard drive or even another computer to back up your primary computer. Whatever backup system you choose, it is extremely helpful to have one that runs unattended, meaning that you don't have to remember to start it. You should also test your backups periodically so that you don't end up with a whole spindle of carefully marked backup CDs that turn out to be blank! An online backup service such as Carbonite can be really helpful if you have a true disaster such as a fire or flood and your computer is destroyed, and a computer that has a RAID (Redundant Array of Inexpensive Disks) system can protect you against a hard drive failure by writing all of your data simultaneously to two separate disks.

8.3 Non-Latin character sets

For translators who work from or into languages that use a Latin character set, it is relatively easy to use software, view web pages, or create, edit and save documents in the non-English language. For translators working from or into languages that use non-Latin character sets (Greek, Russian, Thai, Hebrew, Chinese, Japanese, Arabic etc), the situation can be more complex, and requires more configuration of your computer system. There are three basic ways of implementing a non-Latin character language on your computer.

First, you can use an operating system that is localized for the non-Latin language; for example Red Flag Linux, a Chinese Linux distribution, or the traditional or simplified Chinese version of Microsoft Windows or Mac OS. If you use a localized operating system, all of the text that your computer displays will be in the non-Latin language. This type of setup is a good option for translators who translate into a non-Latin language, or who work in software localization, since it is helpful to see all of the messages generated by the computer in the non-Latin language.

A second option is to use an English operating system with helper kits for your non-Latin language. For example, Apple produces several non-Latin language kits, which enable software such as word processors and web browsers to display and handle input of non-Latin characters.

Finally, advances in Unicode technology have made it possible for many pieces of software to handle non-Latin languages natively, meaning without the use of a helper program. Unicode is a standard that encodes the underlying characters in a language, rather than their visual representations, which enables almost all scripts and writing systems to be displayed on a computer through the use of *code points*, which are numbers that represent a language's characters. In this way, Unicode makes it possible to display languages with non-Latin character sets, including right to left languages such as Arabic and Hebrew.

Before deciding what type of operating system you would like to use, think about what you will be using your computer for, other than standard tasks such as web browsing and word processing, which are now relatively accommodating of non-Latin character sets. Especially if you translate between two languages with different character sets (for example French and Japanese), your needs may be very different from those of a translator who works between English and Spanish. It's also important to research the support offered for your language by the software that you would like to use. If the software has a relatively small market, is it fully localized, with the help files and documentation translated into your language, or is just the user interface localized? If you will be working in software localization, will clients want you to use an operating system in a language other than English? All of these are important items to consider when planning your computer system.

Late model computers have such large hard drives that you might also consider installing multiple operating systems on one machine. You can do this by partitioning your hard drive and having the computer prompt you to select an operating system when you start it up, or by running a virtual machine on top of your normal operating system.

8.4 Speech recognition software

Depending on the type of translation you do and your stamina for typing, speech recognition software is somewhere between totally unnecessary and completely indispensable. For translators who don't mind doing a lot of typing, are relatively fast typists and don't have problems with repetitive strain injuries, speech recognition software is probably not necessary but may help you increase your productivity. If you have poor touch-typing skills, hate typing or have problems with your hands or arms hurting when you type a lot, speech recognition software can be a life-saver. If you frequently work from hard-copy documents, speech recognition software is worth looking into.

Nuance's Dragon Naturally Speaking http://scansoft.com/ naturallyspeaking is the current market leader in speech recognition software. In January 2011 the Preferred edition lists for $299.99 and the Standard edition for $199.98. Speech recognition software has made great advances in the past few years, and it can now be used to perform almost any function that can be performed with a computer keyboard. Nuance claims that the Dragon Preferred edition allows you to dictate your text "three times faster than most people type, with up to 99% accuracy." Note that the "three times faster" claim is based on a typing speed of 40 words per minute, and many translators type much faster than that! Judging by anecdotal evidence from translators who use Dragon, these accuracy rates are quite believable as long as your speech matches what Dragon expects to hear (i.e. you do not have a heavy accent in the language in which you're dictating) and you use the software in a relatively quiet environment.

Speech recognition software can be a boon for translators who type slowly, have problems with repetitive strain injuries or other disabilities. In addition, you don't have to be sitting at the keyboard to dictate, so you can change your position more easily than when you're typing. Translators who use speech recognition software often mention a couple of caveats: dictating becomes tiring over time just as typing does, and dictated texts require careful proofreading because a dictated text does not have any outright spelling mistakes. Whereas proofreading a typed text mostly involves looking for misspelled words (often marked by your spell-checker), proofreading a dictated text mostly involves looking for incorrect homonyms, which may take more time and/or proofreading stamina.

8.5 Text to speech tools

Text to speech tools perform the opposite function of speech recognition software; they read your translation back to you using a computerized voice. These tools can help you get a feel for the sound and flow of your translations by hearing them read out loud. If you have eye problems, you can have the text to speech tool read e-mail or web pages to you so that you're not staring at the screen. One tool that looks promising is Natural Reader http://www.naturalreaders.com, which offers a free version, a Personal version for $49.50 and a Professional version for $99.50 (as of January, 2011). Before purchasing a text to speech tool, make sure to listen to a sample of the voices that come with the software; you may immediately love or hate the default voices!

8.6 Translation environment tools

One of the most frequent topics of conversation among translators is whether to purchase a translation environment tool (also called *translation memory software, computer-assisted translation software* (CAT) or *integrated translation environment tools*), which software works best for a particular application, how much the software costs, and on and on and on.

A very important concept is the difference between translation environment tools and *machine translation software* (MT). A translation environment tool doesn't do the translation for you, rather it helps human translators work faster and more accurately by recycling material that has already been translated and suggesting a match between previous translations and the current one. Machine translation is translation done entirely by a computer. Machine translation has improved to the point that some translation environment tools can now integrate a machine translation engine into their processing flow, so that a sentence (referred to as a "segment" in translation environment tool jargon) from the source document is sent first to the tool's translation memory database of previously translated segments, then if no match is found, the sentence is sent to a machine translation engine before a suggested translation is shown to the translator.

So, on a very basic level, here is how a translation environment tool works: if you translate the sentence "Here is a white cat" and the next sentence is "Here is a black cat," the translation environment tool's translation memory engine will recognize that those two sentences are 80% the same, because only one word out of five is different. The translation environment tool will then show the translator that the only new word in the second sentence is "black," and allow the translator to reuse the previous translation and change only that one word. Most translation environment tools also allow the translator to use an external glossary or a translation memory file that has been created in a different translation environment tool.

By definition, translation environment tools only work with electronic documents; you can't take a piece of paper and run it through the software unless you retype it or scan it first using *optical character recognition software* (OCR), so if you translate mostly from hard copy or scanned documents, translation environment tools are not very helpful. However, most translation environment tools can work with various electronic formats such as spreadsheets, HTML files etc. The translation environment tool works by *segmenting* your source document, meaning that the program breaks your document up into smaller chunks, normally sentences but sometimes paragraphs. Then, when a segment is ready to be translated, the program checks to see if you already translated a similar segment and suggests the match, theoretically resulting in a faster and more consistent translation. This matching feature can be particularly helpful when your translation client has specific terms that they want you to use throughout the document, for example to always use "President and Chief Executive Officer" for the chairman of the company.

Another function provided by most translation environment tools is *alignment*. Alignment means taking the source and target versions of a document, and matching them up so that you have pairs of sentences, one in the source language and one in the target language. This way, you can create a bilingual glossary out of your old translated documents. In practice, this function can be annoying to use; if the source and target sentence pairs don't match up exactly, it requires a lot of time on the translator's part to manually fix the mis-aligned segments.

The use of translation environment tools is somewhat controversial among translators. One reason for this is that translation clients who are aware of the software's capabilities will often ask for discounts on repetitive documents. For example, the client may use the software to analyze a document, and tell you that although the document is 2,782 words, they only want to pay for 2,582, because there are 200 words that are repeated in the document. Or, a client might ask you to reuse the translation memory file from an old translation, and want to pay only for the new words translated; for example if the client is putting out a new version of a software manual, they might want to pay you to translate only the updated parts. Some translators are completely opposed to giving discounts for the use of translation environment tools, on the grounds that they pay to acquire and maintain the software, they do the work on the translation, and even if a segment is a 100% match with a previously translated one, the translator still has to read the segment and sometimes make other adjustments as well. On the other hand, translation agencies and even some direct clients are very familiar with the potential time savings of translation environment tools, and they in turn want to reap some of the benefits. Many translators rightly point out that when there are time savings from using these tools, three players in the situation want to benefit: the translator, the translation agency and the end client, and obviously someone has to forgo his or her percentage of the savings.

8.6.1 Compatibility between translation tools

One issue with translation environment tools is that there are a variety of programs available at different price levels and with different features, and these programs are not always compatible with each other. Many of the most popular programs store data in proprietary formats, and the bilingual files themselves are not often easily interchangeable between tools. Fortunately, the *TMX* (Translation Memory eXchange) and *XLIFF* (XML Localization Interchange File Format) open standards are changing this situation somewhat. Translation memories created in these formats should be interchangeable among tools that support them. XLIFF in particular is a promising standard if the major tool vendors will agree to implement it. XLIFF allows the exchange of not only translation memories, but of the actual bilingual files that translation environment tools produce. In this way, a translator could theoretically switch from one XLIFF-based translation environment tool to another and reuse all of the bilingual files created by the old tool, which would be an enormous asset. Some newer software vendors use these open standards and guarantee that translation memories generated by their software can be reused with other software. It's a good idea to check a tool's support for these formats before you buy the software.

8.6.2 SDL Trados

Trados `http://translationzone.com` is the market leader translation environment tool, and probably the tool most requested by translation agencies. Until 2009, Trados worked from within Microsoft Word for the most common file formats (using a component of Trados known as Translator's Workbench) and in an application known as TagEditor for some less common file formats. In 2009, SDL released SDL Trados Studio which is a standalone application that uses the two-column format (source text in one column, target text in the other) popularized by Déjà Vu and MemoQ. This new Trados release is designed around the XLIFF format and supports TMX (see above for more information on these formats).

Although Trados has a huge market share and can be a good business investment, it is very expensive: in January 2011, SDL's website listed new licenses for Trados Studio 2009 at €845 (US $1,181 at that time) and upgrades from Trados 7 at €230 (US $325). In addition, it is no longer possible to upgrade from a Trados version that is older than Trados 7; if you have an older version, you have to purchase a new, full-price license. These prices (along with the need to learn an entirely new interface in order to use Trados Studio) seem to be leading a growing number of translators to look at other translation environment options. However, many translation agencies still request or require Trados; just make sure that you really need or want the software before you purchase it (or any other similarly priced programs!). Unlike some other translation tool providers, SDL offers very limited free training or support; for example, if you do not purchase SDL's Premium Software Maintenance Agreement (PSMA), you have access only to the SDL Trados Knowledge Base, not to e-mail or phone-based technical support. You can download the SDL Trados Studio demo from TranslationZone http://www.translationzone.com.

8.6.3 memoQ

MemoQ http://en.kilgray.com is produced by Hungary-based Kilgray Translation Technologies, with the slogan "memoQ users have more fun." The first version of memoQ was released in 2005 and the software has quickly gained a strong following in the industry. MemoQ has a free version that allows you to create one translation memory for one document at a time. Licenses cost €99 or $149 for a one-year "translator standard" license and €620/$910 for a full-featured "translator pro" license. Its developers assert that most translators can learn to use 90% of the software's functionality in about two hours. On memoQ's website, you can view screenshots of the program (it uses a two-column format) and find out about memoQ's series of free webinars. Kilgray also offers free training videos, an online knowledge base and e-mail support.

8.6.4 Déjà Vu

Déjà Vu, created by the French company Atril http://atril.com, is very popular with European translators and is becoming more so in the United States. Déjà Vu uses a two-column format and incorporates a number of "wizards" to guide users through major tasks; you can download a free 30-day trial version from Atril's website. This website includes an excellent FAQ (frequently-asked questions) section for those who are new to translation environment tools; as of this writing, Déjà Vu had just decreased its prices to €250 for the standard version and €660 for the professional version. Atril offers an online knowledge base, downloadable manuals and various levels of paid support.

8.6.5 Wordfast

Wordfast http://wordfast.com advertises that it is the second (behind SDL Trados) most widely used translation environment tool in the world. Wordfast has a very good reputation among freelance translators due to its reputation for good customer support (every license comes with a year of access to Wordfast's e-mail hotline) and its policy of allowing unlimited upgrades for three years after you purchase a license. Wordfast has recently forked into two distinct applications: Wordfast Classic which works from within Microsoft Word, and Wordfast Pro which is a standalone application. A license that allows you three years of upgrades on both Wordfast Classic and Wordfast Pro is currently 330 euros.

8.6.6 Heartsome

Heartsome http://heartsome.net, developed in Singapore, is a relative newcomer to the TM industry, but has gained a lot of attention lately. Heartsome uses the XLIFF standard and is currently the only commercial translation environment tool that will run on a Linux computer system and support the OpenOffice.org free office suite's file formats. A Heartsome license is currently $260 for the personal edition and $415 for the professional edition.

8.6.7 OmegaT

OmegaT http://omegat.org is the best-known free translation environment tool. It is developed by a team of volunteers and has a very active user community. OmegaT is a standalone application that does not require Microsoft Word but it can exchange files with other translation memory applications by using the TMX (Translation Memory eXchange) format. And it really is free! OmegaT is compatible with files from the free OpenOffice.org office suite, so you can build a completely free and open source translation system with it.

8.6.8 across

across http://across.net, produced in Germany, is another tool that integrates a translation editor, translation memory engine, terminology system and some project management tools. Like many of the other programs, across offers several editions; the Personal Edition for freelancers is now offered for free.

8.7 Translation memory discounts

Translation memory discounts are a hotly debated issue in the industry. The idea behind them is fairly simple: if a document contains many repeated segments, or is substantially similar to a document that a translator has previously translated, the client may try to negotiate a discounted rate for the repeated words or segments. Whether you agree to this or not is certainly up to you. Following are some arguments on both sides of the issue:

- **In favor of translation memory discounts**: some people feel that a translator shouldn't be paid a full rate to do the same work twice, and that repetitive documents are faster to translate, therefore the translator can offer a discount and still earn his/her usual hourly rate. In addition, translators may feel pressured to offer translation memory discounts simply because other translators do, and they are afraid of pricing themselves out of the market.

- **Against translation memory discounts**: other people feel that since translators pay to acquire, master and upgrade their translation environment software, any productivity advantages that the translator gains belong to him or her. Also, some people feel that in other professions where text is re-used, professionals normally do not give discounts. For example, attorneys generally do not give discounts on wills or other estate documents although they may reuse the same boilerplate document over and over again.

8.8 A word about word counts

Word counts seem like a simple issue, but they aren't. Word counts are the metric upon which a translator's income is based, so an accurate word count is very important. However, counting words is more complicated than it might appear. Different software applications count words differently; for example some programs do not count words in text boxes, headers and footers while others do include those words. Also the source and target word counts for a given document many vary considerably.

The first step in counting your billable words is to agree with your client on whether you will be using the source or target language word count. In languages such as French, German and Spanish, the English word count can be up to 30% less than the non-English count, so this is something to take into consideration. The document format will also affect which word count is used. If your source document is a low-quality PDF, it may be impossible to use the source word count unless you want to (laboriously) hand-count the words.

If there is a default word count standard in the industry, it is probably the word count generated by Microsoft Word. Most translation environment tools generate their own word count, and there are also dedicated tools such as AnyCount http://www.anycount.com/, PractiCount http://www.practiline.com/ and Complete Word Count http://www.shaunakelly.com/word/management/complete-word-count.html. The advantage of a dedicated word counting program is that these programs can count the words for documents in a variety of formats, and can also count an entire folder of files with one click.

The most important element of word counting is to agree in advance about what standard you will be using. This can avoid bad feelings on your or the client's part once it comes time to bill for the job.

8.9 Choosing a computer system

Probably the most popular computer setup for freelance translators is a desktop computer with a Windows operating system and standard software such as Microsoft Office. However, translators do also successfully use Mac or Linux systems as well. While some translation clients will want their translators to run a certain operating system, most clients don't have strong preferences as long as the completed translation files are delivered in the correct format. There are even blogs, websites and forums specifically for translators who use non-Windows operating systems, for example TransMUG http://transmug.com/ for Mac users and Linux for Translators www.linuxfortranslators.org for open source systems users.

If you choose to use a non-Windows operating system, your file formats must be compatible with what your clients require. For example, the free and open source office suite OpenOffice.org www.openoffice.org can reliably save files in Microsoft Office format, but it will not work with software such as Trados 7 or Wordfast Classic that require Microsoft Office macros.

8.10 A bit about machine translation

Machine translation, translation that is done entirely by a computer, has come a long way in the last decade or so. Once the laughing stock of the language industry, machine translation is now extremely powerful and extremely useful for certain types of translation tasks. It's important to avoid comparing machine translation to the work that human translators do, because these two "translators" are suited to completely different tasks. Machine translation is a great option when a translation has to be done fast and cheaply. When a translation is going to be used for publication, distribution, advertising etc., a human translator is an absolute must. Machine translation is really useful for getting the gist of a document, or for producing a "good enough" translation of a huge volume of text in a short amount of time. Instead of fearing machine translation or dismissing it as useless, human translators need to promote machine translation's strengths while also promoting the aspects of translation that only a human can do a good job on.

Machine translation is an invaluable tool in situations where human translators simply can't meet a sudden demand for huge volumes of translation in a niche language. For example, in the aftermath of the 2009 Port-au-Prince earthquake in Haiti, the small number of English<>Kreyol translators simply could not keep up with the volume of information that had to be translated. Several machine translation providers jumped in to help and alleviated the crushing backlog of text messages, e-mails and emergency information. At the same time, it is likely to be many years or even many decades before machine translation can produce high-quality translations of annual reports, advertising materials, website copy and similar types of documents.

Some translation memory programs now integrate machine translation, so that if the program doesn't find a potential match in the database of work that the user has already translated, it will then produce a potential match using machine translation. Some translators love this feature and others hate it, and its usefulness depends on the type of document that's being translated.

8.11 Resources

- Translators Training (video demos and reviews of translation environment tools):
  http://www.translatorstraining.com

- American Translators Association Language Technology Division: http://www.ata-divisions.org/LTD

- TransMUG (Mac Users Group for Translators):
  http://www.transmug.com

- Linux for Translators:
  http://www.linuxfortranslators.org

- Association for Machine Translation in the Americas:
  http://www.amtaweb.org

9 Rates, contracts and terms of service

9.1 Setting your translation rates

Possibly the most anxiety-provoking aspect of launching your translation business is deciding how much to charge. Charge too much and you'll be priced out of the market; charge too little and you'll be working overtime just to make ends meet. The easiest way to remove some of the anxiety from this decision is to gather some objective data such as how much money you would like to make, and how much it will cost you to run your business.

Every language combination and specialization has a range of rates; for example, translators of Asian languages into English will almost invariably earn more than translators of European languages into English, although there are individual translators who will always be the exception to this rule. In addition, how much you need to charge depends on your cost of living. An English to Spanish translator living in rural Mexico can afford to work for lower rates than his or her colleague who lives in Manhattan. Some translators get very angry about these global outsourcing possibilities, but the reality is that they are just a function of the variation in global costs of living; in a developing country, someone earning $15.00 an hour can live quite well, while someone making $75.00 an hour in Geneva may be barely getting by.

Adding to the pricing confusion is that most people are used to calculating their wages by the hour, while most translation projects are paid by the word. Depending on the language combination involved, individual translators will want to be paid either by the source or the target word. For example, Romance languages such as French and Spanish take about 30% more words than English to communicate the same text. So, translators of French or Spanish into English will usually ask to be paid by the source word, whereas translators working in the opposite direction will earn more money by being paid by the target word. If there is an industry standard, it is often to set payment based on the source word count, since this lets the client and the translator know how much the project will cost before it has even begun. For character-based languages such as Japanese and Chinese, the word count is most often based on the number of English words regardless of the direction of the translation.

Beginning translators often don't know how to estimate how long a translation will take, so don't know how to set their per-word rates in order to reach their target hourly rate. Whereas an experienced linguist knows approximately how many words per hour he or she translates when working on various types of documents (general, technical, highly technical, handwritten, hard copy, HTML etc.), there is no way to know this if you haven't done much translation; you simply have to time yourself while you translate to see how fast you work. In general, a translator who is a relatively fast typist (or uses speech recognition software that works well) can translate 400–600 words per hour or 2,000–3,000 words per day, but this is only a ballpark figure. When working on a highly technical document with few repetitions, or on a handwritten document that is difficult to read, even an experienced translator might produce just a few hundred words per hour.

Non-billable time is another variable in the pricing equation. When you have a full-time job for an employer, you are normally paid to work 40 hours a week, whether or not all of those hours are spent working productively. As a self-employed freelancer, you will be paid only when you are actually translating. Tasks like marketing, billing, collections, e-mailing back and forth with current and prospective clients, providing rate quotes for upcoming projects and downtime when you have no work, are all off the clock—work time that you have to put in but that you don't get paid for. When all of these tasks are added up, most freelancers will spend at least 25% of their time on non-billable work, and it's not unreasonable to estimate up to 50% non-billable time when you add in slow times when you would like to be working, but aren't.

9.1.1 Calculating your baseline hourly rate

Completing the following two charts will help you determine how to set your rates for translation. In the *sample* column are example figures to use for comparison. Fill in your own figures in the right-hand column.

Table 9.1: BILLABLE HOURS

	Sample	Your estimate
Hours per week you would like to work	40	
Weeks per year you would like to work (subtract vacation weeks)	48	
Total working hours per year	**1,920**	
Sick hours per month x 12 months	96	
Legal holiday hours (7 days per year)	56	
New total working hours per year	**1,768**	
Non-billable time (25–50% of total: marketing, accounting, etc)	700	
Billable hours per year	**1,068**	

Table 9.2: HOURLY RATES

	Sample	Your Estimate
Your salary goal	$55,000	
Taxes (15–50% of salary)	$14,000	
Internet, website hosting, phone, fax, cell phone (sample= $100/mo x 12 mos)	$1,200	
Memberships and professional development (including association dues, conferences, etc.)	$1,500	
Marketing and advertising (could be much more or less)	$500	
Office rent (no total given since most translators work from home; if you plan to rent office space, write it here)	$0	
Office supplies (envelopes, printer paper, pens, etc)	$500	
Computer hardware and software (depends heavily on what you need to purchase)	$800	
Auto and travel expenses (could be $0 if you never travel for work, or several thousand dollars if you attend multiple conferences or travel to visit clients)	$250	
Total cost of business operation	**$73,750**	
Required hourly rate (Total revenue divided by billable hours from chart above; sample is $73,750/1068)	**$69.00**	

This hourly rate worksheet is a major step in pricing your translation services. Your next step is to determine how you're going to arrive at that hourly rate. In order to do this, you need to know how fast you work (the only way to figure this out is to time yourself while you do some translations) and what the range of rates for your language pairs and specializations are.

9.1.2 Gathering objective data about rates

Before deciding how much to charge for your translation services, it's important to do some research about what other translators charge and what clients will pay for translation in your language pairs and specializations. There are various ways to do this: you can look at rate surveys on popular translation portals such as ProZ www.proz.com and Translators Cafe www.translatorscafe.com (be aware that these are generally slanted toward the low end of the market) or order the most recent compensation survey published by the American Translators Association www.atanet.org, all of which have breakdowns by language pair. Another possibility is to search the Internet for websites of translators who work in your language pair and see if they publish their rates. Depending on whether translators in your language pair are forthcoming with their rates, you might also ask other translators if they will share their rates with you. If you do this, it is very important to avoid antitrust violations by simply asking for factual information, not asking what rates you should charge or what rates the other translator thinks that clients will pay.

9.2 Rate sheets

Whether or not you publish or discuss your rates, it's important to have a rate sheet somewhere, even if it's just for your own use. Your base rate will cover most jobs, but clients will also ask about other types of services, so you should have the following in mind:

Standard rate. This is the rate that you apply to most translation projects that come across your desk. Generally, this would include projects that are in one of your usual areas of specialization, are in a format that you normally handle, and don't involve working overtime to meet the deadline.

Volume discount. Some translators offer a lower per-word rate for larger projects, since a large project allows you to spend your time working instead of looking for work, and decreases your administrative overhead for things like billing and collections. The flip side of this (and why not all translators offer a volume discount) is that in the worst case scenario, a large project can actually cause you problems if you have to turn down work from other regular clients who contact you while you're tied up with the big project. If you are busy all the time at your standard rate, it does not make sense to offer volume discounts. Large projects are also problematic if the client pays late or doesn't pay.

Rush charge. Nearly every translation project is a rush in some sense, but not infrequently something is a real rush. For example a client might ask you to receive a document at 4PM and return it by 9AM, or to work on a weekend, or to translate a 4,000 word document in 24 hours. Normally these jobs are charged at a higher rate than your standard rate, although for a regular client some translators waive their usual rush charges.

Minimum charge. Even if a translation involves only a few words (and these projects come up; for example when a company wants their marketing slogan translated into fourteen languages), you still have to communicate with the client, issue an invoice, deposit the check, follow up if the client doesn't pay etc. For this reason, most translators have a minimum charge of for projects that are under a certain word count, such as $50 for 200 words or fewer.

Editing rate. Most translations that are intended for publication will need to be edited by a second translator. If you are interested in doing this work, you might charge by the word or by the hour for it. If you charge by the hour you will make more money if the translation is a good one but you will be in a real bind if the translation is poor and you've effectively committed to a flat rate. The terms "editing" and "proofreading" are sometimes used interchangeably in the translation industry, but editing generally means checking the translation for errors, omissions and mistranslations by comparing it to the source document, while proofreading generally means reading the target document and finding target language errors. Some translators who work with direct clients have their work proofread by monolingual speakers of the target language who are specialists in the subject area that the document relates to.

Translation memory discounts. Some clients will ask you to discount your rate for repeated words in a document. Whether you do this or not is up to you. Some translators offer no discount at all, others only for 100% matches, still others offer a stepped pricing plan for *fuzzy matches*, for example charging 60% of their regular rate for 75–99% matches, 80% of their regular rate for 50–74% matches and so on.

9.3 Contracts or work-for-hire agreements

Many clients will ask their freelance translators to sign contracts or work-for-hire agreements before beginning work. Make sure that you understand the implications of these documents before you sign them. These contract clauses are mostly applicable if you work through translation agencies. For example, you should carefully consider, possibly with the advice of a lawyer, whether you will consent to terms such as:

- Agreeing not to get paid until the end client pays the agency. Of all the terms that translators are asked to accept, this is probably the most difficult. In one sense, it's understandable that an agency doesn't want to take the risk of having to pay tens of thousands of dollars to translators for a project that the agency itself is never paid for. If a translator returns poor quality work, the agency doesn't want to be responsible if the end client refuses to pay. On the other hand, the translator's contract is with the agency, not with the end client. An agency owner should know that he or she is accepting some level of financial risk by subcontracting work. If you agree to this type of clause, it is important to realize that you are accepting some risk of non-payment yourself.

- Agreeing to indemnify (hold harmless) the client against lawsuits and/or claims resulting from your translation. If you sign a contract with this type of clause, make sure that you carry your own professional liability or *errors and omissions* (E&O) insurance in case one of your clients is sued because of an error in your translation. The client should have a quality control system in place so that an error by one translator doesn't have a disastrous effect on the final project, but not every client will have this. This type of contract clause is more of a concern if you work for direct clients, who may be less likely to have your work edited or proofread before distributing it.

- Agreeing not to accept or solicit work from the agency's clients. Most intermediaries between end clients and freelancers, not just translation agencies, require this type of *non-compete* agreement. It's perfectly reasonable to ask that you not go behind the agency's back and ask the end client to hire you to translate for them directly. However, unless you and the agency compare your client lists (something the agency will probably be unwilling to do), it is difficult or impossible for you to comply with this clause.

- Agreeing not to subcontract work to another translator. This is another fairly common and reasonable clause; just make sure to abide by it if you sign it.

- Agreeing to abide by confidentiality standards. Especially if you work in legal, financial or patent translation, you will probably come into contact with trade secrets, confidential financial information that has not been released to shareholders and other types of information that cannot be disclosed. If you sign a contract with this clause, it is important to read and abide by its provisions For example, financial translators might be required to agree not to engage in insider trading as a result of their knowledge of a company's financial information before it is released to the public.

- Agreeing to submit to a credit check, criminal background check or financial review in order to be bonded. Like the confidentiality agreement described above, there are good reasons why some translators have to be bonded. For example if you work with a bank's clients' financial information, or translate information about a mutual fund's identity verification procedures, you have access to information that might allow you to steal money from the company or its clients. In order to be bonded, most insurance or bonding companies will investigate your financial records and/or criminal background. Just make sure you are clear on what you're agreeing to when you sign this clause, and that you understand what information the bonding company is going to collect or ask for. If you have a criminal record, make sure you understand what types of charges, arrests or convictions must be reported.

If you find a clause in a contract that you don't want to sign, you have a few options. You could cross out the clause in question, modify it or refuse to sign the contract completely. Whether or not this is successful depends on the client. Some agencies will agree to a change, others will refuse to work with you if you don't sign their contract. The most important thing is to realize that if you sign a contract, its terms are legally enforceable, even if an agency employee tells you, "I can't imagine we would ever really enforce that..." If the client wouldn't enforce the clause, it shouldn't be in their contract.

9.4 Terms of service

Just as a client or potential client may ask its translators to sign a contract, so you as a translator may ask your own existing or potential clients to agree to your terms of service. *Your agreement with the client should first summarize the project, per-word rate, whether the word count is based on the source or target count, the project deadline, the file format and the delivery method.* Even with a client that you work for regularly, you should always summarize the basic elements of the project so that everyone is in agreement before you start work. With a regular client, this would probably take the form of an e-mail confirming the project's due date and rate, along with any special instructions. Make sure to confirm the time zone that the deadline applies to, for example 10 AM U.S. Eastern Time, not just 10 AM.

With a client you have never worked with before, you may want to ask the client to agree to your own terms of service. Following are some sample terms to consider:

- *No claims will be considered after X days from the date of the invoice.* You need to set a time frame within which the client can ask you for revisions, tell you that there's a problem with the translation etc. You don't want a client coming back several months later to complain about a project that you barely remember working on, but you do need to give the client time to review your translation. So, a time limit of somewhere between two weeks and one month is probably reasonable.

- *Within the limits of the law, all claims will be limited to the amount of this invoice.* A clause such as this lets the client know that if they're not satisfied with your work, the most they can do is refuse to pay you; they can't, for example, ask you to forgo your own payment *and* reimburse them for the cost of additional editing of your translation. However, especially if you translate for direct clients, there may be situations where the client is legally allowed to sue you for damages if they are sued as a result of errors in your translation. Make sure you are clear on this before accepting work from direct clients.

- *The client's terms of service are not in effect until approved in writing by the translator.* This prevents the client from holding you responsible for abiding by a contract that you haven't signed. For example, the client cannot come back to you after the project and say, "Our translator contract specifies that you don't get paid until the client pays us."

- *If the client is employed by an end client or third party, the translator's business agreement is with the client only. The client must pay the translator as agreed upon, regardless of the end client or third party's payment policies.* In essence, you are letting your client know that if the end client doesn't pay them, they still have to pay you. The end client is not *your* client if you work with an agency.

- *The translator retains copyright to the translation until the invoice for the translation has been paid in full.* Very important! When you contract with a client to do a translation for hire, you give up your copyright to the translated work, unless the contract specifies otherwise. However, if the client never pays you or doesn't pay in full, they haven't upheld their end of the work-for-hire agreement. Basically, this clause gives you the option of pursuing the client or end client for copyright violations if they use your translation without paying you.

- *If the translation project is canceled after a project assignment has been made, the translator will be paid for all work completed up to the time of cancellation.* Sometimes a client will send you the wrong file, cancel a project or scale a project down in size after you have already started working. While you shouldn't expect to be paid for the entire project unless you've completed it, you should be paid for the part of the work that you've already done. With a reputable client this shouldn't be a problem as long as the reason for the cancellation is clearly the client's mistake.

- *If the client is not satisfied with the translator's work, the translator must be given an opportunity to correct the translation before payment terms or rates are changed.* No matter how skilled you are as a translator, some clients will not be fully satisfied with your work. This type of clause will (hopefully!) protect you against clients who say that they're not happy with your work and will not pay you, or clients who take a unilateral discount on the agreed-upon price. Before the client brings up any change in the agreed-upon payment terms, they should let you know specifically what is wrong with the translation and give you the chance to correct it.

9.5 Questions to ask before accepting a project

Especially when you first start out as a translator, it is very important to ask some key questions before you accept a translation project. If you are contacted by an agency that you have never worked with before, your first step should be to see if the agency is credit-worthy. You can check a translation client rating service such as Payment Practices www.paymentpractices.net while you are on the phone with the agency or before you respond to their e-mail, so that you can see what their reputation is before you accept the job. In addition, you should ask the prospective client for more information about the translation, including:

- What is the subject matter of the translation?

- When is the deadline? (Make sure to specify the time zone and clarify potentially vague terms such as "end of day" or "close of business")

- How many words or pages long is the document?

- What format is the document in (for example, PDF, Word, HTML, handwritten etc.)?

- Does the client want you to use translation memory? If so, will you apply a translation memory discount, or charge the same rate for the entire word count?

- Are there any special instructions? (For example use of a glossary, certain formatting specifications, etc.)

- And of course clarify the rate for the project!

9.6 Researching your potential clients

As we'll discuss later in this chapter, occasional problems with clients are unavoidable. No matter how well you set things up in advance and how well you know your clients, issues will come up and you'll need to resolve them. In the case of payment and contract issues, the best defense is definitely a good offense; it's infinitely easier to lay the groundwork correctly for a project than to chase after a client for your money, or lose a valuable client because of a misunderstanding.

The most important first step in making sure you get paid is to know who your client is. Dealing with someone who gives you only an e-mail address or cell phone number as contact information is a setup for non-payment, since you will have no recourse if the cell phone number or e-mail address in question is discontinued when you need to get paid. At the very least, you should get every client's full name or business name, website address, mailing address (if the address is a P.O. box, ask for a physical address as well), and phone and fax numbers.

If you're suspicious about the client's legitimacy, this information should let you do at least a brief search; for example you could Google the client, call directory assistance and see if the phone number you get matches the phone number the client gave you, etc. If the client has a website, you can also find out the information that the client provided when they registered their website domain name. This is public information; the easiest way to do this is via a website such as Whois.Net http://whois.net, where you can enter the client's domain name and immediately find out who the technical and billing contacts for the domain are. For this reason (the ability to trace a client through a third party), it is also wise to beware of clients who will only provide you with a free e-mail address, for example Hotmail, Yahoo or Gmail. Although free webmail services are very convenient, one of the unfortunate attractions of these free accounts is that you don't have to provide any verifiable information about yourself to get one. Thus it is very easy for someone to use a free e-mail address and then cancel it and simply disappear, which is much harder if your e-mail account is through a paid Internet service provider who has your contact and billing information. For clients who are established businesses or large translation agencies, you also have the option of doing a credit check on the client through a credit bureau such as Experian http://experian.com or Equifax http://www.equifax.com.

Another truly excellent way to investigate potential clients is via a translation industry payment practices list. The oldest and largest is Ted Wozniak's Payment Practices http://www.paymentpractices.net. A membership to Payment Practices is $20.00 per year, but will easily pay for itself if you avoid working with even one untrustworthy client. On this list, and others like it such as the ProZ Blue Board http://proz.com/bb (available only to paying members) and Translator Client Review http://www.tcrlist.com you can post a query about a potential translation client, and other translators will respond to you and tell you their experiences working with this client. Based on the information given, the client will receive a score; on Payment Practices the score is on a one to five scale with five being the best rating. Payment Practices assigns two separate ratings: one for payment reliability and one for the translator's willingness to work with the client again. Client rating services are mostly applicable if you work with translation agencies, but sometimes you will get responses about direct clients as well.

It is also acceptable and even advisable to ask a potential client for references from other translators who work for them. You might be uncomfortable or feel impolite doing this the first few times, but it's important to remember that if you work for a client who promises to pay you when the project is done, you are *extending credit* to the client by working without an up-front payment. Since you cannot resell the translation somewhere else if the client doesn't pay you, you are effectively loaning the client your time for the promise of future payment. Don't do this lightly; set the situation up so that you have the best possible chance of getting paid.

9.6.1 Handing potentially problematic clients

Problems can arise when you research a client and find out either that the client has a reputation as a non-payer, or that you can't find much information at all about the client. In this situation, a translator who is very busy and is not actively looking for new clients will probably just refuse the project being offered. However, a beginning translator may want to assume more risk in order to secure a large or interesting project with a new client.

There is no reason not to let the client know your concerns; after all, you're basing your concerns on objective and widely available information, not on rumor and hearsay. If the client is a known non-payer, it is unwise to work for them unless they will pay in advance. You might tell the client that "due to translation industry payment practices ratings of your agency, any work I do for you will need to be paid in advance." It is unlikely that an insolvent client will agree to this, but it is probably worth a try if you really want the project. However, make sure that the payment is completed using a method that is immediately verifiable, such as a money order or a PayPal transfer.

With a client that doesn't have much of a track record, such as a newly established agency, you need to make more of a subjective judgment call. You could ask if the client will pay in advance, or for a large project you could ask if the client can pay part of your invoice when you deliver part of the translation so that you are protected from a complete loss in the event that the client is insolvent.

9.6.2 Recourse against non-paying clients

At some point in his or her career, nearly every translator does business with a client that either cannot or will not pay. There are a few last resort tactics that can be used with this type of client. First, make sure that you have sent the client a first, second and final collection notice and that the final notice was sent by certified mail with a return receipt. In addition, you need to be sure that you have ironclad documentation of your arrangement with the client, for example an e-mail specifying the project due date, rate of payment and payment terms.

Once your final notice has produced no response, it is unlikely that the client is willingly going to pay you. However, there are still a few possible avenues of recourse, including:

- Posting a report of your experience to translation industry payment practices websites such as Payment Practices, Translator Client Review and the ProZ Blue Board. As long as you stick to the factual elements of the experience, this is a perfectly acceptable thing to do, and it is also perfectly acceptable to let the non-paying client know that you are doing this.

- Hiring a collection agency. Members of the American Translators Association can use the services of Dunn & Bradstreet for collections, and there are various other collection agencies that will, for a percentage of what they collect, pursue the non-paying client for you. Some collection agencies have a minimum charge, and this option is probably best reserved for large invoices.

- Contacting the end client. If the non-paying client is a translation company or other intermediate party and you know or can find out who the end client for your translation was, raising the possibility of contacting the end client for payment can be an effective tool. If the end client has paid your client, you may be able to leverage the possibility of contacting the end client and informing them of the situation.

- Taking the client to court. If the client lives in your area, a small claims court case may be a good option; check with your local court system to find out the procedure.

- Chalking it up to experience. There are very few freelance translators who go their entire careers without ever encountering a non-paying client. If you research your clients before working with them, agree in writing on the project deadline, rate and payment terms, you may still have to pursue a client for payment every so often. Just as even the best stores have to deal with shoplifters and fine restaurants have the occasional customer leave without paying, you need to factor an occasional deadbeat client into your overall business planning.

9.7 Payment terms and methods

Before beginning a translation job, it is important to establish when and how you are going to get paid, especially because payment terms and methods vary widely between clients and countries.

In the United States, the most common payment terms are net 30, meaning that the client will pay the full amount of your invoice within 30 days of when you submit the invoice. Most United States-based clients pay by check in dollars, although some will also pay by electronic bank transfer (often referred to as *ACH* for Automated Clearing House) or by PayPal.

Outside of the United States, payment terms may be longer; for example net 60 or even net 60 from the end of the month, meaning that the invoice is paid 60 days from the end of the month in which you submit it. Before working for a client whose payment terms are long, it is important to consider how long you can wait to receive your money. Especially for a large invoice, you need to plan carefully in order to be able to wait two to three months to be paid.

9.8 International payments

When you work with a client located outside your home country, you need to clarify not only the payment terms, but how the client will pay you. There is no one perfect method for international payments, and each method involves various fees to either the translator, the client or both. Following are some possible methods by which international clients may pay you.

9.8.1 Wire transfer

Probably the most common method for payments that United States-based translators receive from international clients is wire transfer. A wire transfer is initiated by the international client from an account in the client's currency and the money arrives into the translator's American bank account where it is automatically converted into dollars. On the positive side, wire transfers don't require any special setup beyond giving your client your bank account identification information. The United States does not widely use the IBAN system (which assigns your account a unique number, like a phone number) so normally you give the client your account number, the bank's routing number and the bank's SWIFT code, which you can obtain by calling your bank. Wire transfers are also very secure and fast.

The major disadvantages of wire transfers are banking fees and exchange rate losses. Banks normally charge for both outgoing and incoming wire transfers, and the charges may be as low as $5.00 or $10.00 to as much as $50.00 per transfer depending on the bank. In addition, your bank's exchange rate may be significantly lower than the standard mid-market exchange rate for that day, which will cause you to lose money. Unless you use a large commercial bank, it may also be difficult to find out what exchange rate will be applied.

9.8.2 Foreign currency checks

Some banks absolutely refuse to allow clients to deposit checks in a foreign currency, while others are quite flexible about it. If your bank allows you to deposit foreign currency checks, make sure that you ask about the associated fees and about the time it will take for the funds to be available for withdrawal. If the bank sends the check back to the originating country for collection, it may take a significant amount of time for the check to clear.

9.8.3 Overseas bank accounts

Especially if you have clients who pay in a very strong currency such as euros, an overseas bank account can help you avoid bank transfer fees and exchange losses. For example, if you have a lot of clients in Germany, it could be attractive to have a German bank account that would allow you and your clients to avoid wire transfer fees and could enable you to keep your money in euros and spend it when you travel to Europe. However, this option also has a few negative points to consider. Many countries are reluctant to let non-residents open bank accounts, and some may charge high fees either to maintain the account or to have a debit/credit card associated with it. Translators who have overseas bank accounts also need to consider the tax and accounting implications of having income in multiple currencies and multiple countries.

9.8.4 PayPal

PayPal www.paypal.com is an online payment service that can be a good option for certain types of payments. A personal or basic business account with PayPal is free, but PayPal charges a fee for some types of payment transactions. For example, the sender can fund the transfer either from the sender's own PayPal balance, from the sender's checking account or using a credit card. Make sure to check PayPal's fee structure before you use it to accept payments. One positive aspect of PayPal is that the recipient of the payment can refuse a payment and all of the charges are reversed; so if you receive a payment but the fees are very high, you can simply refuse the payment and ask the client to use another method to pay you. PayPal's fees are normally a percentage of the amount of money that is transferred, so it may be a better option for small amounts of money than for large ones.

9.9 Setting the stage for payment

Maximize your chances of getting paid on time by billing your client in a timely manner and using a well-organized invoicing system. On the next page is an example of what a translation invoice looks like; if your freelance business is incorporated, you will have an *Employer Identification Number* (EIN); if you are a sole proprietor you will need to provide your Social Security number so that the client can issue you a 1099 form if they pay you more than $600 per calendar year.

Sample Invoice

Invoice

Name of Translator d/b/a

Your Business Name here

Street Address

City, State, Zip Code

Phone number

Email address

EIN: XX-XXXXX/SSN: XXX-XX-XXXX

Please make checks payable to: *Your Name or Your Business Name*

Invoice Number: *Include an invoice number that has some logic to it; for example the year and then a reference number (for example 2011-01) or your initials and then a number (JGF01, etc).*

Billed to: *Name of client*

Client Contact: *Name of the person who assigned the project to you*

Date: *Date you are issuing the invoice*

Date due: *Make sure you and the client agree on the payment terms*

Agency Project Number: *Many clients will give you their own job number to include here.*

Description of Project: *Include a short description of the project, such as "Translate market research surveys from English to Spanish"*

Word Count: *Include the number of words, and make sure you and the client agree on whether you are charging by the source or target word count*

Rate: *Include the per-word or per-hour rate here*

Total Amount Due: *Include the total amount the client owes you.*

The easiest way to send your invoices, unless the client has another system, is to send them with the translation when you submit it. This way, if the client received your translation, you know that they received your invoice too. Some clients may want you to invoice them at the end of the month, or to submit your invoice to a special e-mail address just for invoices. If this is the case, just make sure that the client confirms that they received your invoice. Normally, the client is not expected to pay your bank fees (such as a fee that your bank charges when you receive a wire transfer), so don't add these to the invoice unless you have cleared it in advance with the client. Likewise, the client should not charge you for their bank fees (such as the fee that they have to pay to wire money) unless they have cleared it with you in advance.

9.10 When things don't go as planned...

If you haven't received the client's payment within the specified time frame, wait an appropriate amount of time and then politely remind the client that the payment is due. An "appropriate" amount of time is up to you; if the payment terms are net 30, most translators would probably wait one to two weeks before contacting the client. Hopefully the client will respond promptly and tell you that the payment is on its way. If not, you will have to do some conflict resolution.

There are two types of non-paying clients; clients who can't pay and clients who won't pay. Clients who refuse to pay normally withhold their payment on the basis of your translation quality. If or when this happens, it is truly painful to have your translation skills criticized. Remind yourself that the client is already anxious and angry; denying that any problem could have existed will probably only make the situation worse. Before you try to defend yourself, make sure that you followed the client's instructions to the letter. If the client provided a list of terms, make sure that you used them. If the client asked you to format the translation as closely as possible to the original document, make sure that you did this. If the client asked for the document in a certain font, make sure that you used it.

If you are completely convinced that you performed the translation to the client's specifications, ask to see a copy of the edited or re-translated translation so that you can see your real or perceived errors. Then, decide if you think that the client's claim is valid or not. In some cases, this may require going to a third party, such as another translator selected by you or the client, to make a decision as to whether the translation is high quality or not. Although it is sometimes painful to do this, it's important to acknowledge that there is some possibility that the client may be right and that you did a poor quality job; insisting otherwise will probably not lead to a satisfactory outcome for you.

How much you should press the quality issue with the client depends partially on how big the project is. If your fee for the project is only $50.00, it probably isn't worth arguing with the client over whether you did a satisfactory job; with the time it would take to go over the revised translation and submit a list of points that you disagree with, you're probably better off simply letting go of the $50.00. If the project is $5,000 and the client is refusing to pay, it's a different story. As of this writing, there is no industry standard dispute arbitration process for translation; for example the American Translators Association does not intervene in disputes between translators and their clients, so it's up to you as an individual to work things out.

The second type of non-paying client, the client who can't pay, presents more of a challenge. This type of client may start out with excuses that seem reasonable: accountant is on vacation, payment will be made by a certain date, large client is late on paying your client, invoice was lost or never received, or sent to the wrong person or accidentally deleted; but soon these explanations will prove to be untrue. The client may come out and admit that they are having cash flow problems, or may string you along indefinitely, or go out of business and/or file for bankruptcy. The first step with this type of non-paying client is to send a series of three to four increasingly serious reminder letters, known formally as *dunning letters*. You can start out by politely reminding the client of the terms you agreed on and asking them to pay, then escalate the situation to include copies of the letter to higher-ups at the agency or company, then finally threatening to involve a third party. This third-party involvement may be in the form of taking the client to small claims court, hiring a third-party collection agency, or contacting the end client for the translation and letting them know that you were never paid for your work, and that because of this, they may be violating United States copyright law by using your translation. If you send this type of letter, it is very important to consult a sample dunning letter in order to make sure that you are not breaking the law by saying something untrue or misleading. Following are some examples of first, second and final notice dunning letters.

Sample First Notice

Dear *Name of Person who assigned you the project*:

According to my records, I have not received a check for Invoice #_____ for _____ which was due for payment on _____. Please let me know the status of this payment when you have a moment, and thank you again for your business.

Sample Second Notice

Dear *Name of Person who assigned you the project (CC to this person's Accounts Payable Department or Supervisor)*:

I recently contacted you regarding an overdue payment for Invoice #_____ for _____ which was due for payment on_____. As of today I have not received this payment, and I do need to hear from you regarding its status, as the payment is now considerably past due. Please reply to me as soon as possible and let me know the date on which you will be mailing this payment, if it has not already been sent.

Sample Final Notice

Dear *Name of Person who assigned you the project (CC to this person's Accounts Payable Department or Supervisor)*:

```
Despite my two previous notices to you on _____ and _____,
I have not yet received your overdue payment for Invoice
#_____ in the amount of _____.  You have had sufficient
time and notice regarding the status of this payment.
Failure on your part to pay this seriously overdue invoice
by _____ may result in my posting information about this
transaction to translation industry payment practices lists,
referring this account to a third party collection agency,
and/or contacting the end client of the translation in
question to inform them of the non-payment situation.  I
trust this will not be necessary, and look forward to
receiving your payment as soon as possible.
```

If you need to involve a third-party collection agency and you are an ATA member, you can investigate the services of ATA's affiliate program with Dunn & Bradstreet Receivables Management. They handle both U.S. and international unpaid accounts, and normally take 25–50% of what they collect. Other third-party collection agencies exist, but make sure that the agency is legitimate before you hire them; for example call the Better Business Bureau where the agency is headquartered and find out if there have been any complaints against the agency.

If you get to the point of sending dunning letters to a client, there is some possibility that you will never get paid in full. Many translators feel that if more than four months have elapsed since the original payment deadline, the client is probably not going to pay without some serious outside incentive. Dunning letters can motivate a client who is either trying to delay payment, or trying to see who complains most loudly about not getting paid. However, if the client absolutely doesn't have the money to pay you or goes bankrupt, there may not be much you can do if your dunning letters don't get a response. This is further proof that you're much better off investigating the client up front than fighting for months to get your payment after the fact.

9.10.1 Arbitration and dispute resolution

Another avenue to pursue with a non-paying client is *arbitration*, a non-court proceeding involving an independent and neutral arbitrator. Arbitrators are often attorneys, and you may choose to have your own attorney represent you during arbitration. One important element of arbitration is that unlike filing in small claims court, you normally cannot file for arbitration without the cooperation of your non-paying client, since they are usually required to fill out the arbitration submission agreement along with you. For more information, see the website of the American Arbitration Association http://www.adr.org .

9.11 Cash flow issues

Happily, most translators go for long periods of time without ever dealing with a non-paying client. The more common problem is clients who don't pay on time. Some clients only issue checks on certain days of the week or month, so if you contact them on June 10 to let them know that the payment due June 1 didn't arrive, they may not be able to issue a check until June 15. With the time needed to mail the check, you might receive this payment three weeks late.

It's up to you as a freelancer to decide how to deal with cash flow issues. When you have a full time job, it's a pretty safe bet that your paycheck that's due on the 25th will be in your account in time to pay your mortgage on the 1st, but a freelancer would be unwise to take this kind of gamble. This is an important issue to consider before you start working as a freelancer. If you are planning on translation being your primary source of income, make sure that you have enough of a cash cushion that you're not left scrambling when a check doesn't arrive as planned.

9.12 Resources

- American Translators Association model contract:
  http://www.atanet.org/careers/model_contract.php

- American Translators Association compensation survey:
  http://www.atanet.org/publications/index.php

- WikiEducator article on International Finance and Payment Methods:
  http://wikieducator.org/International_Finance/Payment_Methods

- Payment Practices: http://www.paymentpractices.net

- Translator Client Review: http://www.tcrlist.com

- ProZ Blue Board: http://www.proz.com/blueboard

- PayPal: http://www.paypal.com

- XE (currency conversion site): http://www.xe.com

- Currency Online (web-based foreign currency services):
  http://www.currencyonline.com

- Travelex (web-based foreign currency services):
  http://www.travelex.com

10 Growing your business

When you're putting together your first translation resumé and wondering who your first clients will be, it's hard to imagine the day when you'll be turning down work or raising your rates. However, the translation industry is growing fast, so it's important to set your business up to grow as well.

10.1 Managing contacts

One of the most important steps you can take at the start of your business is to log all of the business contacts you make. Over the course of your first year in business, you are likely to come into contact with a huge number of potential clients. Rather than counting on your memory to remind you who these people are, or deleting their "thanks, but no thanks" e-mails, you can save and organize their contact information in order to make use of it later.

There are various ways to keep track of your contacts. You can use a simple index card system or Rolodex, a spreadsheet or a dedicated contact management database. The key element is to keep track of the name of the person you e-mailed or spoke with, all of his or her contact details and what you communicated about. This way, if a potential client tells you, "We only work with translators who have more than three years' experience," you can contact them again when you meet their requirement. If a potential client tells you that they're not taking applications in your language pair right now, contact them again in six months to a year to let them know you're still interested. You can also use this list of contacts to build a mailing list for your own e-newsletter or other promotional tools

10.2 Incorporating and planning for taxes

When you begin freelancing, you will probably pay taxes as a
sole proprietor. Later, you may consider incorporating. Some
translators operate their businesses as sole proprietors for many
years, while others incorporate immediately. It's a good idea to
talk to an accountant about whether incorporating would be a
good idea for you; here are some of the factors to consider when
you think about your business structure.

Separation of finances. Incorporating forces you to keep your
business and personal finances separate, since your clients
pay the corporation and then the corporation pays you
wages, even if you're the only employee. In this way you
are always sure how much the business is earning and how
much you're spending on the business. However, as a sole
proprietor you can achieve the same effect by having a business bank account and a personal one and carefully tracking
the cash flow between the two accounts.

Limitation of liability. Since a corporation is its own legal entity,
incorporating gives you some protection against personal
liability. In most cases, your personal assets cannot be seized
to pay the corporation's debts or legal judgments. If you are
planning to work for direct clients or subcontract work to
other translators, this alone can be a good motivation for
incorporating.

Tax relief. Some corporate structures, such as *S-corporations*, can
save you money on taxes, since an S-corporation's profit is
not subject to self-employment tax. Incorporating may also
allow you to take more tax deductions than you do as a sole
proprietor.

Capital. If you need to raise capital, for instance by taking out a
business loan, it is often easier to do so if you are incorporated. However, so few translators take out business loans
that this is not a major concern.

Expense. Depending on where you live, setting up a corporation may be extremely inexpensive or very expensive. For example, in some states it costs as little as 99 cents to file your articles of incorporation on-line, while in other states the fee may be much higher. Likewise, some states will require corporations to pay a filing fee for their required annual report, while others will not. Incorporating can also result in higher accounting expenses, since some corporation types must file payroll taxes every quarter. For more information on forming a corporation, see your state's Secretary of State website.

Paperwork. Incorporating definitely requires extra paperwork. At the very least, you have to file *Articles of Incorporation* in your state, probably file a *Trade Name Registration* in your state and receive a *Federal Employer Identification Number* that you provide to clients instead of your personal Social Security number. If you hate doing accounting and don't want to hire someone to do it for you, this is definitely a consideration!

If you would like to incorporate, there are various corporate structures to choose from, such as an *S-corporation, C-corporation,* or *limited liability corporation* (LLC). Do some research on your own or talk to an accountant to determine which one is right for you.

Whether you incorporate or not, tax planning is a crucial element of being self-employed, and one that catches many people by surprise. When you have a full-time job, you accept the fact that some of your salary goes to taxes, but you usually don't have to write out a check to the federal or state government for that amount. As a freelancer, you will be responsible for tracking and paying your taxes, normally done four times a year. If you are incorporated, you will probably have to pay payroll taxes, and if you are a sole proprietor you will probably have to file estimated taxes every quarter to avoid owing a large amount plus penalties at the end of the year.

The most important element of paying your own taxes is to meticulously keep track of your income and expenses. Whether you do this on your computer or on paper, it is imperative to write down the date and amount of every payment you receive and every purchase you make for your business, and to save all receipts. The amount of tax you will pay depends of course on how much you earn and your overall tax situation, but it is important to factor the additional tax you pay as a self-employed person into your projections. The self-employment tax, currently 15.3% of your net earnings from self-employment, consists of 12.4% of your income for Social Security, up to a maximum of $10,788.00, and 2.9% of your income for Medicare. The reason these taxes can come as a shock is that when you have a full time job, your employer pays half of these taxes and you pay half; but when you're self-employed, you pay the entire amount. Also keep in mind that you pay the self-employment tax *in addition* to regular income tax, not instead of it.

On the up side, as a self-employed person you have many more opportunities than your salaried friends to reduce your tax burden through deductible business expenses. Here again, it's important to talk to an accountant or tax preparer to find out what is deductible in your particular situation. However, most self-employed translators can deduct home office expenses, computer hardware and software, Internet and phone costs, travel expenses, professional association memberships, continuing education, office supplies, business-related travel, professional journal subscriptions, books, dictionaries, even meals out that are work-related.

Following is a brief overview of the basic business entity types to consider; but note that these business entities are regulated in the U.S. by individual states rather than at the federal level, so be sure to research the laws of the state you live in.

C-corporation. Many large businesses are C-corps, but small businesses can choose this structure as well. One of the major advantages of a C-corp is that it allows you to deduct 100% of your health insurance premiums as a business expense. C-corp profits below $50,000 are also taxed at a lower rate than a comparable amount of taxable income.

S-corporation. This is possibly the most popular structure for a one-person corporation. The main advantage of an S-corporation is that as long as you pay yourself a "reasonable wage" (as defined by the IRS), you can pass some of the corporation's income on to your individual tax return, which can avoid you having to pay self-employment tax on it. For example, if you have net income of $60,000 and pay yourself wages of $30,000 (which are subject to self-employment tax), you can then pass the additional $30,000 on to your individual tax return as profit, where it is subject only to regular income tax, not self-employment tax. One disadvantage of an S-corp is that all shareholders must be U.S. citizens or permanent residents; nonresident aliens cannot be S-corp shareholders.

Limited Liability Corporation. The "Single Member LLC" is probably the second most popular corporate structure for freelance translators. Like an S-corp, an LLC is a flow-through entity, allowing you to pass profits and losses on to your personal tax return. In addition, LLC owners may be nonresident aliens. In some states, LLCs have a limited duration, for example 30 years or less, so if you are incorporating early in your career, be sure to investigate this in your state.

Sole Proprietor. A self-employed person whose business is not incorporated is referred to as a sole proprietor. Being a sole proprietor has its advantages, including very little administrative overhead. In many states you do not even need a business license to operate as a sole proprietor, and all of your income is simply reported on Schedule C of your individual tax return. However as a sole proprietor, you have no liability protection in the event of a lawsuit or financial claim (meaning that at least in theory, your personal assets can be seized), and all of your income is subject to self-employment tax.

10.3 Obtaining health insurance

Many people worry about how to obtain reasonably priced health insurance when they are self-employed. As a freelancer, your options depend on where you live, what your health history is and whether you have access to group health insurance through a family member's job. Some of your options are:

- Purchase COBRA coverage through a previous full-time job. Under the COBRA act, your employer is generally required to let you stay on the employer-sponsored health plan for 18 months after you leave your job. You are usually required to pay the entire premium yourself, but COBRA can be a good option if you would have difficulty obtaining another policy.

- Purchase group health coverage through a family member's job. If your spouse or partner has a salaried job and has access to an employer-sponsored health plan, that may be your most affordable option. This is especially true if you have a pre-existing condition because health insurers are normally required to cover all of a business' employees at the same premium rate regardless of their health histories.

- Purchase an individual health insurance policy. This is probably the most prevalent option among freelancers but the cost and hassle can vary considerably. Some states have guaranteed issue laws which mean that health insurance providers must cover everyone who wants to purchase coverage. This can be a plus if you have a pre-existing condition but can make coverage more expensive for people who are healthy and low-risk. If your state allows health insurers to sell catastrophic coverage plans (for example, plans that cover only inpatient hospital care), they may be quite affordable as long as you have savings to cover routine care. The major unknowns when you apply for individual coverage are how much the coverage will cost and what factors the health insurer will consider when deciding whether to accept or decline you. Anecdotally, some freelancers pay as little as $300 per month for a high-deductible policy that covers an entire family while others pay over $1,000 per month for a policy that covers just one high-risk person. In addition, many individual health insurance plans have a waiting period to cover pre-existing conditions and may either exclude maternity coverage or require you to purchase a maternity care rider.

- Join your state's high-risk insurance pool. Most (but not all) states have a government-sponsored health insurance option for people who have pre-existing conditions or whose health histories make them uninsurable on the open market. Check your state's division of insurance website to see if this type of coverage is available where you live.

- Apply for health coverage as a group of one. Some states classify self-employed people as "groups of one" and require health insurers to cover them just as they would cover the employees of a larger business. Again, check your state's division of insurance website to see if this is an option in your state.

10.4 Raising your rates

At some point in your translation career, you'll realize that your translation experience or specializations can command higher rates than what you're currently charging. Also, you might be interested in either earning more money or in working less, so you might need to charge more at some point.

Unfortunately, the answer to the question, "How do I get my existing clients to pay me more money?" is almost always, "You can't." Most often, the best way to raise your rates is to look for new, higher paying clients. For example, if you've worked for a translation agency for two years, making 12 cents a word, your client might be willing to go along with a rate increase to 14 cents a word, but it's highly unlikely they'll agree to pay 25 cents a word. In some easily outsourced language pairs such as English into

Spanish, there may even be pressure on translators to decrease their rates over time. On the other hand, if you land a direct client who is used to paying 30 cents a word for translation through an agency, your offer of 25 cents a word may strike them as the best deal they've gotten all year. You simply have to eliminate your lowest paying clients and look for higher paying ones to replace them.

One of the best strategies for raising your rates is to look for clients who themselves earn a healthy income, or orient yourself toward higher-earning specializations. Not surprisingly, business sectors that are big earners in the U.S., such as law, financial services and pharmaceuticals, are correspondingly well-paying for translators who work in those areas. So, part of the key to raising your rates is to find clients who can pay what you'd like to earn, and show these clients that your services will help their business run faster, more effectively or more profitably.

10.5 Ten ways to please a translation client

The easiest way to keep your translation business profitable is to cultivate a core group of regular clients who will fill your in-box with translation projects, allowing you to spend your time working rather than looking for work. Implementing some of the tips below will help you keep a regular stream of work coming your way.

1. **Meet every deadline.** If you can't consistently meet deadlines, you're not well-suited to being a freelance translator. Remember that your clients have deadlines too, and are sometimes waiting for your work as part of a larger project. As one experienced translator comments, "8:00 means 7:50, not 8:10."

2. **Be easy to reach.** Put your contact information in your e-mail signature file, so that a client never has to look up your phone or fax number. Realize that many times, if clients cannot reach you immediately, they will contact another

translator. Since over 90% of contacts from clients will be by e-mail, put an auto-responder on your e-mail if you will be out of the office for even a few hours.

3. **Follow directions.** While it can be time-consuming to follow many different clients' particular ways of doing things, you will save the client time and money, and thus get more work from them, by following their instructions to the letter. If the client asks you to put your initials in the file name, do it. If the client asks you to put the word "Invoice" in the subject line of the e-mail containing your invoice, do it.

4. **Don't waste your clients' time.** It's acceptable, and even encouraged to ask questions when you need to clarify something. However, it's also important to show respect for your clients' time, and for the fact that yours is probably not the only project they are handling. Keep your e-mails short and to the point, and make your questions clear and easy to answer.

5. **Provide referrals.** Many translators worry that providing referrals to other translators in the same language combination will lead to less work for themselves, but in fact the opposite seems to be true. Clients like to work with freelancers who solve the clients' problems, and when you're too busy and can't handle their work or are going on vacation, it's a problem for them. Have the names of two or three translators in your language combination who you really trust, and provide these names to your clients when you aren't available for work.

6. **Be easy to work with.** This isn't to say that you should be a pushover or let clients take advantage of you, but for your regular clients, it's worth putting in some extra effort. Thank them for giving you their business; be friendly and polite if a payment is unexpectedly late; fill in for them in a pinch when another translator lets them down.

7. **Ask for constructive criticism.** It's important to see feed-

back as part of your quality assurance process, not as an attack on your abilities as a translator. If a client asks for changes in your translation, make them politely and immediately; if you decide later that the changes are unnecessary and you don't want to work for the client again, it's another matter. With your regular and trusted clients, periodically ask what you can do to better meet their needs, then implement these changes.

8. **Appreciate your clients.** Your regular clients are the people who make it possible for you to earn a healthy income while living a flexible and self-directed freelance lifestyle. A small gift at the end of the year is always appreciated when a client has given you regular work.

9. **Don't bicker.** If a prospective client offers you a project at a ridiculously low rate, politely decline it, possibly sending them a copy of your standard rate sheet if you have one. Don't insult them for offering such low pay or make negative comments about their business; just courteously decline to work for them and let them move on to someone else.

10. **Charge what you're worth, and earn it.** There will always be another translator out there who is willing to work for one cent per word less than you are, so don't compete on price alone. Giving your clients high-quality work every time proves that their investment in you is a good one.

10.6 In conclusion

Striking out on your own and launching a freelance business can be equal parts thrilling, intimidating, overwhelming and educational. Working for yourself can give you the chance to make your own decisions in a way that most people are never able to do. Whether your business succeeds or fails, the responsibility will be yours!

Be prepared for your first year as a freelancer to be an intense one. In addition to doing the actual work of translating your clients' documents, you'll be learning how to market yourself, network with colleagues, keep your accounting records, work productively without a boss, avoid working too much or to little and much more. At the end of your first year, reward yourself for surviving and take a realistic look at what you've achieved, then set high but achievable goals so that your second year will set you firmly on the path to long-term success.

If you get discouraged about your prospects as a freelance translator, remember that if you have excellent language skills and you are a good writer in your native language, there are clients who need you. By almost any measure, the translation industry is growing faster than most industries, so the work is out there if you market yourself assertively. Set measurable marketing goals and you will start to get some work; do an excellent job on that work and more will follow. Remember to keep marketing yourself even when you have enough work, so that your work pipeline is always full. And have fun! Translation is a stimulating, enriching and fulfilling profession that can provide you with a very healthy income and enough time to pursue your non-work interests too. There are niches in the industry for people in all types of language combinations and specializations, so there's likely to be a niche for you!

10.7 Resources

- U.S. Internal Revenue Service tax information for corporations:
  http://www.irs.gov/businesses/corporations/index.html

- Kaiser Foundation state-by-state health insurance data:
  http://www.statehealthfacts.org

- U.S. government state-by-state guide to incorporating:
  http://www.usa.gov/Business/Incorporate.shtml

- Freelance FactFile (general freelancing information):
  http://www.freelancefactfile.com

- Freelance Folder (general freelancing information): http://www.freelancefolder.com

Resources

U.S. Government agencies employing translators and interpreters

Central Intelligence Agency

The CIA http://cia.gov offers a number of opportunities such as Foreign Language Instructor, Language Specialist, Foreign Media Analyst and National Clandestine Service Language Officer. Requirements and salaries vary, but most positions are full-time and the largest number of opportunities is in the Washington, DC area. Applicants must be U.S. citizens and willing to complete a medical and psychological exam, polygraph interview and background investigation.

Federal Bureau of Investigation

The FBI http://fbi.gov offers salaried Language Analyst positions as well as full-time or part-time Contract Linguist positions. Positions are located at the FBI's Washington, DC headquarters or at regional Field Offices. Applicants must be U.S. citizens and willing to complete a polygraph interview and background check. Language Analyst applicants must be willing to travel on temporary assignments for 30 days at a time.

State Department Office of Language Services

The State Department http://state.gov employs staff translators and interpreters and maintains a roster of freelance translators and interpreters. Application is by competitive examination; interpreter candidates must be willing to travel internationally for at least three weeks at a time.

National Security Agency

The NSA http://www.nsa.gov is especially interested in hiring Language Analysts for Asian and Middle Eastern languages, but employs translators and interpreters in a variety of languages. The NSA also administers the Language Enhancement Program, which re-trains French, German, Italian, Portuguese, Russian or Spanish linguists to work in Asian and Middle Eastern languages.

Associations for translators and interpreters

American Translators Association

The ATA http://atanet.org is the largest association of translators and interpreters in the U.S.; offers its own translator certification exam to members, publishes the monthly *ATA Chronicle*, and organizes a wide range of professional development activities including an annual conference. The ATA website also lists numerous local ATA chapters.

National Association of Judiciary Interpreters and Translators

NAJIT http://najit.org is a professional association for court interpreters and legal translators. Publishes a quarterly journal, *Proteus*, and organizes an annual conference. Website includes helpful information about the court interpreting profession.

Translators and Interpreters Guild

TTIG http://ttig.org is the only nationwide labor union of translators and interpreters. Offers a translator and interpreter referral service as well as other membership benefits in cooperation with the Newspaper Guild–Communications Workers of America.

American Literary Translators Association

The American Literary Translators Association http: //literarytranslators.org is a professional association for translators of literature in all languages. Publishes a newsletter and the *Translation Review*, website also includes a list of university-level literary translation programs.

International Association of Conference Interpreters

Membership in the AIIC http://aiic.net is open only to experienced conference interpreters who are sponsored by current AIIC members. However, website includes helpful information for those who would like to pursue conference interpreting opportunities.

Selected training programs and home study courses for translators and interpreters

In general, translator and interpreter training programs are not language courses, and applicants are expected to have a high degree of fluency in English and at least one other language before applying. Most colleges and universities and even some community colleges and adult continuing education programs offer foreign language skill development courses. For a list of translation degree and certificate programs that are approved by the American Translators Association to fulfill its education and experience requirement for translator certification candidates, visit the *Certification* section of atanet.org. For more information on translator and interpreter training programs, see the publication *Park's Guide to Translating and Interpreting Programs in North America*, published by the American Translators Association.

Monterey Institute for International Studies

Located in Monterey, California, Monterey Institute http://miis. edu offers graduate programs through its Fisher Graduate School of International Business, Graduate School of International Policy Studies, Graduate School of Language and Educational Studies, and Graduate School of Translation and Interpretation, as well as intensive language courses. As of this writing, candidates for the two-year M.A. degree in Translation, Translation and Interpretation, or Conference Interpretation must have fluency in English and at least one of: Chinese, French, German, Japanese, Korean, Russian or Spanish.

Kent State University Institute for Applied Linguistics

Located in Kent, Ohio, the Institute for Applied Linguistics http://appling.kent.edu offers undergraduate and graduate translation degrees; a B.S. in Translation and an M.A. in Translation. Current language combinations offered by the program include English paired with French, German, Japanese, Russian or Spanish.

University of Hawaii at Manoa Center for Interpretation-Translation Studies

The CITS http://cits.hawaii.edu does not offer a degree program, but conducts a summer certificate program for translators and interpreters who work in English paired with Japanese, Mandarin Chinese, or Korean. During the school year, the CITS offers a General Skills Training program for translators and interpreters.

Logos free online translation theory and practice courses

Logos http://logos.it is also a language services provider and offers two free self-paced translation courses on its website. One course covers general translation theory and practice, and one course covers literary translation. Although the courses do not provide any practice exercises or feedback, they are excellent starting points for beginning translators.

Bellevue Community College

Located in Bellevue, Washington, BCC http://bcc.ctc.edu offers the only translation and interpretation certificate programs in the Pacific Northwest. Language combinations depend on student demand, and students can take courses toward either a certificate program, or for continuing education.

Brigham Young University

Located in Provo, Utah, BYU http://byu.edu offers a B.A. degree in Spanish Translation.

Rutgers University Department of Spanish and Portuguese

Located in New Brunswick, New Jersey, Rutgers University http://span-port.rutgers.edu offers a Certificate of Proficiency in Spanish-English and English-Spanish translation, which may be taken on its own or in combination with an M.A degree in Spanish.

Southern California School of Interpretation

With campuses throughout California and Nevada, Southern California School of Interpretation http://interpreting.com specializes in short (4–11 week) courses to prepare students to take State and Federal interpreter certification exams.

ACEBO interpreter training products

ACEBO http://acebo.com offers the popular home study course *The Interpreter's Edge*, which helps court interpreters prepare for certification exams. The tape set is currently available in a generic (non-language specific) version, or for English paired with Spanish, Cantonese, Mandarin, Korean, Vietnamese, Polish, Russian, Japanese, Portuguese or Arabic.

Florida International University

Located in Miami, Florida, Florida International University http://w3.fiu.edu/translation offers a certificate in Spanish/English translation studies and a certificate in Spanish/English legal translation and court interpreting.

Binghamton University Translation Research and Instruction Program

Located in Binghamton, New York, this campus of the State University of New York http://trip.binghamton.edu offers a certificate in translation, an M.A. in comparative literature with a concentration in literary translation, and a Ph.D. in translation studies.

The Graduate School of the College of Charleston

Located in Charleston, South Carolina, the Bilingual Legal Interpreting Program http://cofc.edu (not offered during the 2006–2007 school year) offers both a Master's degree and a certificate program in English/Spanish bilingual legal interpreting.

American University

American University http://american.edu, located in Washington, DC, offers certificate programs in French, Russian and Spanish translation.

New York University School of Continuing and Professional Studies

With both on-site (New York, New York) and online courses, NYU http://scps.nyu.edu offers a certificate in Arabic, French, German, Spanish or Portuguese translation, paired with English. Courses in German to English, English to Portuguese and Arabic to English are offered online only.

The National Center for Interpretation at the University of Arizona

Located in Tucson, Arizona, NCI http://nci.arizona.edu offers training for Spanish court and medical interpreters, and through its Agnese Haury Institute for Court Interpretation, offers a three-week intensive Spanish/English court interpreter training program every summer.

University of Wisconsin at Milwaukee

UWM http://uwm.edu offers both an M.A. and a graduate certificate in French, German and Spanish translation.

The University of Geneva School of Translation and Interpreting

Known worldwide for training high-level translators and conference interpreters, the ETI http://unige.ch/eti (School of Translation and Interpreting), located in Geneva, Switzerland, offers programs in German, English, Arabic, Spanish, French, Italian and Russian translation at the undergraduate, graduate and certificate levels.

Middlebury College Language School

In business for nearly 100 years, the Middlebury College Language School http://middlebury.edu/academics/ls, located in Middlebury, Vermont, is not specifically geared toward translation, but offers intensive summer classes in Arabic, Chinese, French, German, Italian, Japanese, Portuguese, Russian and Spanish. Students must commit to speaking only their target language for the duration of the program, and the Language School also offers graduate programs overseas.

Bonus preview: Thoughts on Translation

Here's an advance look at *Thoughts on Translation*, a book-length compilation of entries from my blog of the same name. The book will be released in 2011 and will feature over 150 posts from the first three years of *Thoughts on Translation*, loaded with tips on the translation industry, becoming a translator and running a successful translation business. Check Lulu.com or Translatewrite.com for the exact release date and purchasing information!

Paid by the word or paid by the hour?

At a recent American Translators Association conference, I overheard a few conversations about how the translation industry would be affected if translators started billing by the hour rather than by the word. In some cases and for some jobs, translators do bill by the hour, but the tried-and-true per-word charge is still the norm. Here are a few thoughts on charging by the word versus by the hour.

Pricing translation by the word has some advantages: Especially if you charge by the source word, everyone knows up front how much the translation will cost, down to the cent. No surprise overruns to deal with and no estimating how many hours a project will take. Per-word pricing encourages translators to maintain their skills and technology, since efficient translators effectively earn more per hour. In some sense, per-word pricing may also drive translation technology innovations, since translators may be more likely to purchase a tool that allows them to work faster. Also, skilled and efficient translators can probably earn more by charging by the word than clients would be likely to pay by the hour. Say that you're translating 600 words an hour at 14 cents a word; I'll venture a guess that those same clients might balk at paying $84 an hour for translation. Per-word pricing also allows translation buyers to compare apples to apples when it comes to costs, rather than weighing a higher per-hour quote from a translator who claims to work faster versus a lower per-hour quote from someone who works more slowly.

But then again... Pricing by the word has an obvious disadvantage from the translator's side, which is that you are agreeing to work for a flat and fixed rate. So, when you get to those three pages of barely legible handwriting, or the document that's been scanned, faxed and photocopied eight times before arriving in your inbox, you have to decide whether you need to negotiate a higher per-word rate. This can be a particular problem when it comes to editing, which is why I normally decline to be paid by the word for editing.

So then maybe pricing by the hour is better?: Well... yes... no... maybe! The main advantage of pricing by the hour is that there is no risk of loss on the translator's part; if you charge $50 an hour and you work ten hours, you make $500. If you charge 20 cents a word and think you can translate 600 words an hour but the nature of the document is such that you really translate 250 words an hour, you've just taken a big hit. However, my main reasons for continuing to believe in pricing by the word are: a) the client knows up front how much the translation will cost and b) I think that most experienced and efficient translators can earn more by the word than what most clients will pay by the hour. Just don't forget to agree in advance on whether the billable word count is source or target!

Translating official documents

Over the years, I've observed that many translators are somewhere between lukewarm and downright scornful of translating individual clients' official documents: birth certificates, educational transcripts, diplomas, drivers' licenses–you get the picture.

I think that a lot of experienced translators view this as "beginner's work" or not worth their time, so they take it off their range of services. Official documents are not a huge component of my freelance business, but they do total a few thousand dollars of income every year for me and the work is painless and gratifying. Here are a few reasons I think it's worth including official documents in your range of services, and a few tips on how to do it successfully.

Translating official documents is appealing because:

- It's lucrative. Admittedly, translating birth certificates is not a lot of things: it's not creative, it doesn't cry out for stylistic greatness… but it can pay up to a dollar a word and nearly always pays at least 50 cents a word because the standard billing unit is per page. In addition, official documents are a market that agencies really don't want because the size of the projects does not justify their overhead, so freelancers are most individual clients' best option.

- It's gratifying. People who are applying for green cards, graduate school, marriage licenses etc. are really, really grateful to find someone who is experienced and professional to work on their documents.

- It's easy to schedule. When you're translating a driver's license, it's not as if you're juggling other commitments in order to fit in 10,000 words. Most official document translations take less than an hour to complete, so they're easy to schedule.

- The clients pay in advance, so you have no follow-up or collections hassles. I require all individual clients to pay in advance by PayPal or by check, so that I do not have to deal with any after-the-fact invoicing.

And a few tips for setting your official document translations up for success:

- Set a per-page fee and a notarized certification fee; it makes your life and your clients' lives easier. Because of the time it takes to format official documents (especially diplomas and any kind of official certificate), I think that the per-page rate is important. In addition, if you get a lot of inquiries from people who want quotes, it can be helpful to put up a web page with your standard rates, turnaround time and procedures.

- Require advance payment. I cannot stress this enough; you do not want to be chasing after someone for $50, and most official document projects are small enough that your clients should not object to paying in advance. I know that a lot of people complain about PayPal, but I really like it. You receive your money immediately, any difficulties with the actual payment process are between your client and PayPal, and you can use PayPal's free invoicing tool to set up an invoice template that looks professional and does all of the calculations for you.

- Find a free or low-cost notary. My bank provides free notary services to anyone who has accounts there, so my fee for the notarized certification simply reflects the time it takes to go obtain the certification.

In closing, I also think that there are a lot of opportunities to market your official document translation services. International credentials evaluation services, consulates, language schools, international exchange programs and other similar organizations could probably use your services.

Testing the direct client waters

Translators have a variety of reasons for choosing certain types of clients: some prefer agencies for their steady workflow and layer of "insulation" between the translator and the end client, some prefer direct clients for their higher rates and higher degree of autonomy, and still other translators mix up their workflow or work with clients who don't fit exactly into either one of these categories.

In talking to beginning and experienced translators alike, I've noticed that many translators are very intimidated by the idea of working with direct clients. While I think that there are valid reasons to continue working with agencies, I also think that adding some direct client work to your freelance pie is a great way to increase your income and your job satisfaction. If you're interested in dipping at least one toe in the direct client pool, here are a few tips.

- Start small and don't fail out of overambition. In my admittedly unscientific research, I think that many translators aim too high when they enter the direct client market. Don't think Fortune 500, think of other one-person businesses or businesses with very small projects. As you succeed at these projects, trade up!

- Start with projects you can translate in your sleep. If you have a targeted specialization, you know what I'm talking about (for me, it's real estate leases and articles of incorporation). Eventually, you can aim for direct client work that demands creativity and thoughtful turns of phrase. At the outset, look for clients who will have the types of documents you've translated hundreds of times. This will raise your confidence level and increase the odds that the clients will be thrilled with your work.

- Look locally. Especially with direct clients, it's great to have a contact or introduction. If this isn't an option, I think that a friendly "I'm a translator in the area and I'd like to offer you my freelance services…" is a good substitute. In addition, I think that despite the globalization of the professional services market, many small businesses still feel more comfortable working with someone local.

- Track your clients' preferences. In my experience, direct clients don't often have style guides and sometimes haven't really thought about style at all. Do yourself and your clients a big favor by creating a style preferences file for each client. Whenever the client sends you a comment, i.e. "We always refer to our CEO as Chief Executive Officer," or "We use European format for dates even when they're in English," record it in the client's style file.

- Don't undersell yourself. One of the obvious draws of working with direct clients is money. My average direct client pays almost double what my average agency client pays, and my direct clients are usually very low-maintenance; it's a great situation. When you send a quote to a direct client, remember that if the client is a good fit for you, you're offering them more personal service than they would get from an agency, one point of contact instead of many layers between the client and the translator (if the client can even communicate directly with an agency's translator) and more consistency than they're likely to get from an agency. For this, you need to charge real money or you will appear unprofessional.

- Ask for feedback on every translation. "Let me know if you have any specific questions or comments or if there is anything I can do to better meet your needs..." is one of my standard lines. You could even create a simple online survey that your clients could fill out anonymously. Also, you should ask every satisfied client whether you can use their name in your marketing materials and whether they would be willing to provide a testimonial about your work for them.

Glossary

American Translators Association	*Known by its initials, ATA, the largest organization for translators and interpreters in the United States.*
alignment	*The process of pairing source and target documents to create a database of bilingual sentence pairs.*
back-translation	*A translation of a translation, translating the target text back into the source language.*
bilingual	*In the translation industry, a term often used for a person who is a native speaker of two languages.*
CAT tool	*Computer-assisted translation tool; a piece of software that helps a human translator work faster and more consistently be recycling previously translated material. Also referred to as a translation memory tool or translation environment tool.*
certified translator	*Normally, a translator who has passed the American Translators Association certification exam, although this designation is sometimes used for various other credentials, such as having completed a translation certificate program.*
cleaned file	*A file containing only the target language text, with the source text and translation memory program codes removed.*

197

computer-assisted translation tool	*Often referred to as* CAT tools, *this software, under ideal circumstances, helps a human translator work faster and more consistently by recycling text that has already been translated and suggesting possible matches with text to be translated.*
dominant language	*The language in which a person is most comfortable speaking or writing. This may be the person's native language, or, in the case of a person educated primarily in a country where his/her native language is not spoken, may be different from the native language.*
EOM	*End of month, often used in combination with payment terms such as* 30 days EOM, *meaning that the translator will be paid within 30 days from the end of the month in which an invoice is issued.*
FIGS	*French, Italian, German and Spanish, the most commonly translated languages in the United States.*
heritage speaker	*In the U.S., a person who learned a non-English language by being exposed to it at home.*
interpreter	*A person who has a high degree of knowledge in two or more languages and changes spoken words from one language to another.*
invoice	*A statement from a translator to the translation client or translation agency, listing the services the translator performed and the amount that is owed for the services*
language pair	*The two languages in which a translator works.*
literary translator	*A translator who works with novels, stories, poems or plays.*

localization	*The process of adapting a product, piece of software, or text document for use in another target market. This may involve translation, converting units of measurement, adapting graphics, and other processes.*
machine translation	*Translation done by a computer.*
Net 30	*The most common payment terms in the U.S., meaning that the translator will be paid within 30 days of an invoice being issued.*
Non-compete agreement	*An agreement stating that a translator will not seek business from a translation agency's clients for a certain period of time.*
Non-disclosure agreement	*Often referred to as an NDA, an agreement stating that a translator will keep certain pieces of information confidential.*
native language	*A person's first language, which may also be the person's dominant language, or, in the case of a person educated in a country where their native language is not spoken, may be different from the dominant language.*
passive bilingual	*A person who has excellent comprehension of a language, but speaks or writes the language poorly.*
per-word rate	*The amount of money that a translator is paid for each word translated.*
project manager	*A person who coordinates the administrative aspects of a translation or localization project.*
register	*The level of formality or informality in a piece of writing or speech. A translated document should be written in the same register as the source document.*
source language	*The language from which a translation is done.*

source text	*The text from which a translation is done.*
specialization	*A subject area in which a translator has in-depth knowledge; for example a former accountant might specialize in financial translation.*
target language	*The language into which a translation is done .*
technical translator	*A translator who works with scientific, computer or engineering materials. Sometimes used to mean a non-literary translator, regardless of the translator's specializations.*
terms of service	*The conditions under which a translator or translation agency will provide services.*
translation agency	*A company serving as an intermediary between a translation client and a translator, often adding services such as project management, proofreading, and desktop publishing.*
translation memory tool	*Often used interchangeably with* computer-assisted translation tool, *a TM tool creates a database of previously translated text that can be used again.*
translation unit	*The "chunks" into which a translation memory program or CAT tool breaks a source document; normally a translation unit is one sentence.*
translator	*A person who has a high degree of knowledge in two or more languages, and changes written documents from one language to another.*
TMX	*Translation Memory eXchange, an open standard for the exchange of translation memories.*
uncleaned file	*A file containing the source and target translation units, along with the tags inserted by the translation memory program.*

word count   *The total number of words in a document, which may be based on either the source or target text, and may be calculated using a variety of methods.*

Index

About the author

Corinne McKay, CT is an ATA-certified French to English translator specializing in legal and international development translations; she holds a B.A. in French and English from Geneseo
College and the University of Grenoble, France and an M.A. in
French Literature and Culture from Boston College. She has
been a full-time freelance translator since 2002 and is the current
(2008-2012) president of the Colorado Translators Association and
the chair of the American Translators Association's Public Relations committee. In 2006, Corinne published the first edition of
How to Succeed as a Freelance Translator, which has since become
a widely-cited reference for the translation industry with over
4,000 copies in print. Corinne's blog *Thoughts on Translation* is
a lively discussion forum for freelance translators from around
the world and was selected as one of Lexiophiles' top 100 language blogs for 2010. Corinne lives in Boulder, Colorado with
her husband and daughter and enjoys spending her free time
skiing, hiking and biking in the Rockies. Her professional website
is http://www.translatewrite.com.

Colophon

This book was produced entirely with free/open source software
running on Gnu/Linux. The text was written and typeset with
LyX in the Palatino font.

CPSIA information can be obtained at www.ICGtesting.com
228215LV00001B/7/P